Crescent Color Guide to
DOGS

Crescent Color Guide to
DOGS

Angela Sayer

Crescent Books
New York

Photography by Angela Sayer
(Tony Stone Associates: front cover, endpapers,
title spread and pages 15, 17, 23, 35, 40, 47, 61, 80.
Bruce Coleman Ltd—Hans Reinhard: back cover
and pages 12, 27, 52 bottom, 63 left).

Copyright © The Hamlyn Publishing Group Limited 1980
First English edition published by
The Hamlyn Publishing Group Limited
London · New York · Sydney · Toronto
Astronaut House, Feltham, Middlesex, England
Library of Congress Cataloging in Publication Data

Sayer, Angela.
□ Crescent color guide to dogs.

□ 1. Dog. breeds. 2. Dogs. 3. Dogs-Pictorial
works. I. Title.
SF426.S29   636.7'1   80-65948
ISBN 0·517-31853-9

This edition is published by Crescent Books,
a division of Crown Publishers, Inc.
b c d e f g h

Phototypeset by Tradespools Limited, Frome, Somerset
Printed in Italy

Contents

The
History of the Dog

The dingo is said to have descended from the hunting dogs of the Aborigines, and is Australia's sole surviving wild carnivore.

The domestic dog of today is part of the family *Canidae* which also embraces the wolves, jackals and foxes. All are carnivorous with a typical pattern of dentition comprising forty-two teeth in their powerful jaws. The thirty-seven species of the *Canidae* may be broadly divided into dog-like and fox-like types. The wolves, jackals and dogs of the first group are distinguished by having quite distinct foreheads, and smooth or slightly bushy tails. The eyes are fairly round and have circular pupils. In the second group the foxes have the forehead and nose forming a straight line, the tail is generally very bushy, or brush-like, and the pupils of the eyes are oval or slit-shaped. All members of the dog-like group can interbreed and produce fertile offspring, and controlled matings have been under-taken, usually with a male wolf and a female dog. However, the dog-like group and the fox-like group cannot interbreed. All the *Canidae* are digitigrade, having five toes on each of the forefeet and four on each of the hindfeet. The claws are blunt and non-retractile. Members of the dog family are distinguished by their keen senses of sight and hearing, but most hunt by scent; in their wild state, some species live and hunt in well-ordered packs, adhering to strict rules of social order.

The fossil record of the dog family is far from complete, but it is known that it shared a common ancestor with cats, bears, raccoons, weasels and hyaenas – a small but tenacious early mammal called *Miacis* which lived during the Oligocene period, about 40 million years ago. When *Miacis* eventually became extinct, it left behind three groups of descendants, one of which produced the ancestors of the dog tribe and their allies. In this group, fossil remains of *Cynodesmus* in North America and *Amphictis* of Europe are quite numerous and have been found in rock strata formed in areas of open plain. Slightly larger than *Miacis* with longer limbs and more specialized feet, with modified fifth toes, these ancient dog-like mammals had become running hunters, able to catch prey in the open. The lengthening of the limbs was an important adaptation for running, but it is not clear whether or not these animals had begun to run on their toes, instead of on flat feet. Animals closely related to the dog, including the bears and raccoons which diverged from the same ancestral stock about 25 million years ago, are flat-footed to this day. A fossil canine from 20 million years ago in the Miocene era is *Tomarctus*, which lived in North America. It had even longer legs and the feet were very compact, with clear indications that it walked on the tips of its toes. This mammal was about the size and shape of the foxes of the present time.

Eventually, over millions of years, the wolves, jackals and foxes appeared, and although the exact origins of the domestic dog are somewhat obscure, it is generally believed that four wolf origins can be traced. From the Northern or Common Wolf, *Canis lupus*, has probably descended the Northern group of dog breeds including the Huskies, Samoyeds, Elkhounds, Collies, Alsatians and Terriers. The dingo group may have come from the small, pale-footed Indian Wolf, *Canis lupus pallipes*, which lives in comparatively small packs, and rarely howls. The Greyhound group is said to have come from an especially fast subspecies of *Canis lupus*, while the Mastiff group of dogs, including the bulldogs, and their offshoots, such as Setters, Pointers and Hounds, are more likely to have descended from the Tibetan Wolf, *Canis lupus chanco*, or *laniger*. It is of course quite possible that the wolves, jackals, foxes and dogs have another, as yet undiscovered common ancestor, from which they all evolved, separately, in various areas of the world.

It is probable that the first domestication of animals began about 10,000 years ago, when nomadic groups of Paleolithic hunters began to tame the wolves, jackals and wild dogs which scavenged for food scraps around the campsites. In those days, such animals ranged over very wide areas and existed as many separate and varied races. Like the members of the human race at that time, they lived in family groups, necessary for survival, and competed with man for the same sort of prey. Both man and wolf-dog were opportunists by nature, and soon came to appreciate the obvious advantages of coexistence.

From fossil evidence it would appear that early man hunted by driving herds of prey over the edges of cliffs, killing more meat than he could

The close working bond between the shepherd and his dog is constantly reinforced during their long hours of companionship.

The dog in Alaska often has a dual role, being as effective as a guard as it is efficient as a member of the sled team.

handle. This probably attracted packs of dogs in the first instance, which stayed to scavenge on the camp's discarded scraps. Over a very long time period, a hunting relationship would have developed between dogs and man and as the Ice Age retreated and large forests grew, the dog would have proved invaluable in hunting out large animals from the dense cover of the trees. It was during this era that man began to cultivate the ground and learned to grow and harvest grains such as wild wheat and barley, which led to the formation of the first human settlements. The dog's ability to warn of the approach of strangers was soon realized and the animal's role as guard was appreciated and developed. The earliest settlement sites have been found in western Asia; these showed signs that sheep and goats may also have been domesticated, so it is possible that the dog used its skill of herding animals.

Bones discovered in Danish Mesolithic settlements, dated about 8000 B.C., showed that there were two kinds of domesticated dogs at that time, one slightly larger than the other, and both now known as Maglemose dogs. Some more remains, found around the lakes of Switzerland and dating to 4000 B.C., also show the presence of more than one type of dog, the 'Lake' dog, built for running and hunting, and the 'Peat' dog, more probably used for herding. Although not all naturalists agree, it is possible that the first of these dogs is the ancestor of the Spitz group of today, while the second has given us the Pinschers, Schnauzers and Terriers.

By 3000 B.C. four distinct types of dog are known to have existed, the Greyhound and Saluki from Arabia and Africa, the Mastiff from Tibet, the Pointer and the Spitz. General trade routes and tribal migrations spread these breeds through Asia and Europe and they were interbred to produce dogs for specific purposes. The Ancient Egyptians deified their dogs and went into mourning when their pets died, having the bodies embalmed and buried with special ceremonies. Egyptian wall paintings dated at 2000 B.C. show Greyhounds, Pointers, Mastiffs, Terriers and slim, short-coated hounds. Obviously highly prized and revered, these dogs undoubtedly provided some of the root stock of today's breeds.

Gundogs

The gundogs of today are descended from two distinct groups of hunting dogs from medieval times. The first group was used in falconry when active dogs of medium size, and possessed of good game-finding noses, were employed throughout Europe, Asia and North Africa to flush birds from the undergrowth, to be taken by the hawks. These dogs were known as Spaniels, or Hounds for the Hawk. The second group were called 'couchers', from the French word *coucher* meaning 'to lay down', and were used to find partridges and quail which were then driven into long nets. These dogs were the ancestors of our modern Pointers and Setters. The introduction and gradual evolution of firearms increased the efficiency of hunting for food and for sport, and while Pointers and Setters were still in demand for walking up game, the art of retrieving became a necessity. Powerful dogs had been used for retrieving deer shot by archers during the fourteenth century, but in later times Spaniels were taught to bring in shot birds, and any dog that showed particular skill at this was called a Retriever.

Eventually gundogs were selectively bred for specific purposes, and today the breeds each have their particular roles in sporting circles. RETRIEVERS were developed for the special role of accompanying the 'gun', walking or sitting quietly at heel until instructed to fetch a dead or wounded bird, bringing it back, unmarked, to its handler. The various types of Retriever are all built on similar lines and are large active dogs with good heads and strong necks. Their jaws are strong enough to carry even the largest of birds but at the same time so gentle that they are able to carry an egg to their handler.

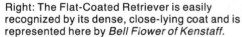

Below: *Stonehealed Gay Lady Jane*, a gentle Golden Retriever of mature years, and typically responsive and obedient.

Right: The Flat-Coated Retriever is easily recognized by its dense, close-lying coat and is represented here by *Bell Flower of Kenstaff*.

The LABRADOR RETRIEVER is one of the kindest and most gentle of all dogs and is a fairly recent breed, first mentioned in 1822 when they were seen in Newfoundland, working with the fishermen. The dogs were used from small boats, and their role was to swim ashore pulling the ends of the large nets which enclosed the fish. The Labrador Retriever of today is an active, powerfully built dog with a short, dense coat of straight, weather-resistant hair. The head is broad but clean cut and there is a pronounced stop between the brown or hazel eyes. The coat colour was originally black, but gradually yellow dogs appeared and proved very popular, then more recently an unusual chocolate shade was accepted. The most distinctive feature of this breed is the very characteristic tail which resembles that of an otter, being thick at the base and gradually tapering to the tip; there is little or no feathering and it is unlike the tail of any other breed of dog. An ideal gundog, this breed's quietly efficient manner and its readiness to learn new skills have made it a popular choice in other spheres, and it has excelled in police and army work, as well as guiding the blind.

Above: The kind Labrador Retriever makes an ideal gundog.

Left: Performing its traditional role, the trained dog returns game to the 'gun'.

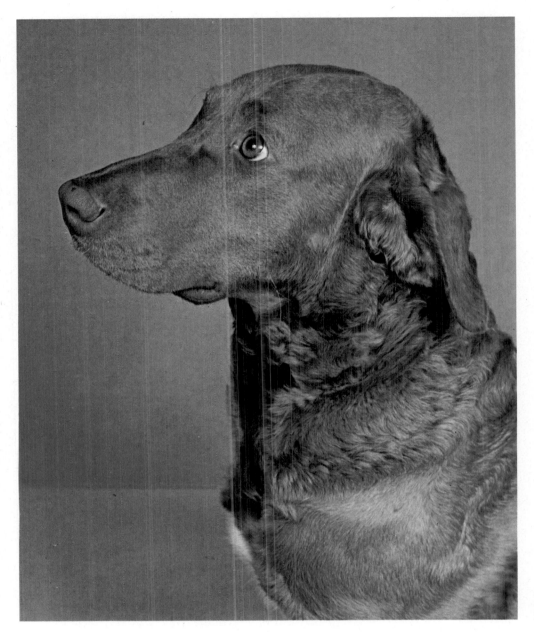

Arna? Bay Abbey, a sedge Chesapeake Bay Retriever.

The CHESAPEAKE BAY RETRIEVER was developed in Maryland, U.S.A. from a pair of Newfoundland dogs, shipwrecked off the coast in 1807. It is a large, bold dog with a rigidly waved and naturally oily coat. This repels water, and so makes the breed ideal for hunting in adverse weather conditions, and for retrieving gamebirds from cold waters. Said to be the oldest member of this group is the large and quite heavily boned black or liver coloured CURLY COATED RETRIEVER, which has remained virtually unchanged since 1860 when it was introduced as a fine dog for retrieving game from water. Popular in Australia and New Zealand, it has a uniquely protective coat of crisp curls.

The GOLDEN RETRIEVER is the result of carefully planned, and meticulously recorded, breeding programmes started by Lord Tweed-mouth in 1868. The first cross was between a yellow wavy-coated retriever and a liver-coloured Water Spaniel, and the offspring line-bred, but introducing outcrosses from time to time, including black retrievers, an Irish Setter and a sand-coloured Bloodhound. The distinctive coat of this breed may be any shade of cream or gold, and may be flat or waved but not curly, with plenty of feathering on the legs and tail. It requires regular grooming to keep it in good condition. This dog's wide-set eyes are golden brown, with a gentle expression.

Once called the Wavy, the FLAT-COATED RETRIEVER is extremely handsome and an excellent and steady worker. Taller and leaner than the Labrador, it is thought to have been specially bred for retrieving, using Newfoundland foundation stock and an admixture of Setters and Spaniels in the early crosses. Today this breed is regaining popularity, having undergone something of a decline over the past few years.

Red Irish Setter
puppies enjoying their
outing in the
countryside.

The Pointer and Setter breeds were developed for a specific role. When out with a shooting party, the Pointer or Setter ranges over the area until it gets a distant, airborne scent of birds. It comes immediately to a complete halt in a rigid stance known as the 'point', seemingly unable to move until either the birds fly or the hunter with the gun approaches them. The trance-like state of the Pointer or Setter has been in-bred and once the dog is on staunch point it cannot move until some sudden noise, such as the click of the gun's safety catch or the sound of the shot being fired, breaks the spell. Once the gun has fired, or the birds are up and away, the dog returns to normal and comes to heel by his handler. Pointers and Setters may also be taught to retrieve, but this is not part of their orthodox work.

The POINTER is a big dog, symmetrical and well-muscled, exuding powers of speed, strength and endurance. The head is fairly long with a pronounced stop between the large, intelligent eyes, and the ears are set high, of medium length, thin and silky. The long muscular neck is set into sloping shoulders. The chest is deep and the back is strong. With good bone, the legs are long and sturdy, and the Pointer's tail is left undocked. The short coat is predominantly white with coloured markings of liver, lemon, black or orange. Occasionally a tri-coloured dog is seen, and even more rarely, one that is completely black. The Pointer is thought to have originated in Spain and was carefully bred, by selecting stock with high head carriage, long legs and light bodies for galloping over grasslands, stubble and moors, plus wide nostrils and superior scenting abilities for finding gamebirds. Easy to train, he also makes a good companion or friendly housedog.

The GERMAN SHORT-HAIRED POINTER is heavier boned and has a shorter more powerful neck, indicating his dual role, being used not only for pointing, but also for retrieving game. He may be either solid liver, or any combination of liver with white, spotted or ticked.

An Engish Setter is easily trained and trustworthy. A good family pet.

The IRISH SETTER evolved in the eighteenth century from setting Spaniels and is the smallest of the Setters. Two varieties are found: the usual Red, which is a deep mahogany colour, and the very rare Red and White, which is only seen, occasionally, in Ireland. Probably one of the most graceful and aesthetically pleasing of all breeds, the Irish Setter has a penchant for tireless effort and staying power that belies his elegant appearance. Being a big dog, it needs plenty of room and is best suited to life in the country and a big garden. There is nothing coarse about this dog, yet the fine long coat covers an efficient well-muscled frame. The head is long with a square muzzle and has a pronounced stop between the dark hazel or brown eyes. The legs and tail are heavily feathered.

The ENGLISH SETTER is built on very similar lines to the Irish, but is a little larger in build. It is a white dog with coloured flecking all over the body in orange, blue or lemon. Tri-colours are also found. Carefully bred by Edward Laverack, from a pair purchased in 1825, the Setter typifies the English country scene and is a quiet and elegant dog, easy to keep and handsome with his fine, long and silky coat.

The GORDON SETTER is the largest of the group and was bred to work on the rugged Highlands and moors of Scotland. Said to have originated in the late 1770s, this Setter was first bred by the fourth Duke of Gordon, who is reputed to have crossed a black and tan collie with one of his own setters in the first instance. Over the years the large but graceful dog developed as we see it today, intelligent, bold and always willing to work. The Gordon Setter must be very well balanced with a strong, short and level back. The head is fairly long too, and has a clear stop before the dark brown, intelligent eyes. The ears are set low and are long, silky and smooth. The coat is of shining black with rich chestnut markings over the eyes, on the muzzle, the throat and inside the legs. The hair is short and fine on the back, the head and the front of the legs, and long elsewhere, flat and feathered.

A protective but gentle and proud Irish Setter and her puppies.

SPANIELS are primarily concerned with the finding and flushing of crouching birds or other game. The Spaniel hunts about close to the handler, minutely exploring every clump of cover so that all game in a particular area is systematically flushed out within easy aim of the gun. The dog then drops until told to go after the dead or wounded bird, which it returns to its handler.

The ENGLISH SPRINGER is perhaps the most common of the Spaniels, a medium sized, keen and active dog, found in black and white, liver and white, or either with the addition of tan markings. The WELSH SPRINGER is similar but less leggy and a smaller dog all round, with a distinctive red and white coat. The ENGLISH COCKER is a compact dog, surprisingly heavy and muscular for its size. It has a narrower head than other Spaniels but a fine nose with extremely good powers of scenting, and may be any solid colour without white, or white with black, liver or lemon markings. The AMERICAN COCKER is smaller than the English variety and has a full long coat with heavy feathering which may be of any colour from buff to black, including red and silver.

The CLUMBER is very distinctive and has a large heavy head and short legs. He makes a particularly good retriever and is easily trained. The white coat has lemon coloured markings mainly on the head and freckled over the muzzle. Orange markings are also permitted but not sought after. Another large spaniel is the SUSSEX, which has a strikingly coloured coat of rich golden liver, each hair shading to pure gold at the tips and causing the dog to sparkle in the sunlight. A slow worker, he is very methodical in the field and often gives tongue in a deep melodious voice when on the scent of game. The FIELD SPANIEL may be of any self colour with the addition of tab markings, and his build makes him particularly good for working in heavy going, while the IRISH WATER SPANIEL, with his coat of unique crisp ringlets, comes into his own whenever there is bogland or marsh to be flushed.

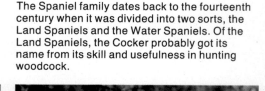

The Spaniel family dates back to the fourteenth century when it was divided into two sorts, the Land Spaniels and the Water Spaniels. Of the Land Spaniels, the Cocker probably got its name from its skill and usefulness in hunting woodcock.

Left: A liver-and-white German Wire-haired Pointer called *Matilde vant Staring Land to Wittekind.*

16

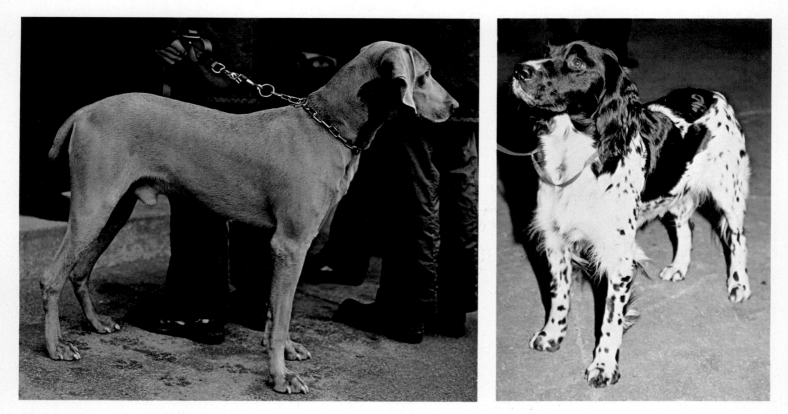

Thor, a Weimaraner working dog used by London's Metropolitan Police.

The Large Münsterländer. A spirited and attractive member of the gundog group.

The LARGE MÜNSTERLÄNDER is a multi-purpose gundog and is the ideal animal for use in rough shooting. Very affectionate and eager to learn, he is easy to train and works willingly and well. Similar to a setter in shape, but with the added strength of the retriever, this dog is well proportioned, and has a coat of long dense hair, feathered on the legs and tail. The head must be black, though a white blaze, snip or star is allowed, and the body is white with black patches, flecks or ticks, in any combination. Another good all-rounder is the HUNGARIAN VIZSLA, a lively and very handsome smooth-coated dog, always russet gold in colour and with dark golden expressive eyes. Described officially as a medium sized hunting dog of noble appearance and lean musculature, he is an aristocratic looking animal and a fine gundog. The Vizsla not only points correctly, he is capable of clean retrieves from land and water and performs his work with quiet and controlled enthusiasm.

The WEIMARANER was first developed in Germany during the nineteenth century, by selectively interbreeding several indigenous and carefully chosen dogs. The court of Weimar sponsored the breeding programmes, and in 1907 the dog was referred to as the Weimar Pointer. The object of this breeding exercise was to produce a perfect all-round gundog, that would not only hunt small game but also the larger forest animals, and the big strong dog with its exceptional nose became a reality. Eventually, breeding pairs were allowed out of Germany to the United States. In the 1950s, some dogs arrived in Britain where the breed has proved very popular, not only as a gundog but in the show ring, and as a good companion and housedog. Nicknamed most aptly 'the Grey Ghost', the Weimaraner is a striking silver grey all over with a slightly lighter shade on the head and ears. The body often shows a distinct dark dorsal stripe along the spine, and the entire coat emits a metallic sheen. The rather spectral effect is completed by the eyes which are often light blue-grey, or occasionally pale amber with an intense, intelligent look.

There are other, rarer breeds of gundog too, mostly bred from the basic types to perform some specialized function, or to expand their range as all-round workers. Most of the gundog breeds make really excellent housedogs and are protective but gentle with children, as well as being clean and tidy in their habits. They need firm training in their first year and a certain amount of discipline, to which they respond with affection and obedience; but if they are not used for their main purpose, they must be given adequate regular exercise.

Hounds

A red-and-white
Basenji champion
dog, *Kingsway Bit of
Class*.

Man has always hunted animals, firstly for food in order to survive, and
many years later for sport, and long before the invention of the gun he
enlisted the help of his dogs. Over the centuries certain types evolved,
through careful selection, which form the basis of the Hound Group of
today. This group is a very large and diverse one and includes two quite
distinct types of hounds, those that hunt by scent, and those that hunt by
sight. Hounds that hunt by scent usually do so when running in packs.
They are generally built on sturdy lines and have great powers of stamina
and endurance. Strong hearts and lungs, and large muzzles with broad
noses enable them to trace elusive scents, and to follow the lines of their
quarries for hours if necessary. Some scent hounds are trained to kill at
the end of the hunt, while others are taught to track down then keep the
prey at bay, giving tongue until the hunter arrives to spare or dispatch the
victim.

Hounds that hunt by sight are built on quite different lines, needing
short, sharp bursts of speed and acceleration rather than long and
sustained effort. Generally long, lean and graceful, some of these sight
hounds have remained virtually unchanged since ancient times. Despite
their sporting role, some hounds settle down well in the domestic
situation and make excellent but extremely energetic pets. Lovers of the
hound breeds maintain that no other dogs supply so much enjoyment,
excitement and sport in return for so little basic care. However, hounds
have certain inbred characteristics which must be understood, and need
sensible treatment and plenty of exercise.

The BASSET HOUND has ancient origins, having been used to hunt for wolves and badgers in France during the sixteenth century. Its name was derived from the word *bas*, meaning low, or near to the ground, and is descriptive of this large-bodied, short-legged breed. After the French Revolution, many people connected with hunting found themselves in reduced circumstances and a hound which could be hunted on foot instead of from horseback became essential. Traditional pack hounds were too fast, and so a slower breed with shorter legs, increased powers of endurance and extra scenting abilities was developed.

This silver sable dog is a Basset Griffon Vendeen—*Jomil Larbi of Voran.*

Four types of Basset were eventually produced. The first was the BASSET ARTESIAN NORMAND, imported into Britain in 1875, which most closely resembles the short-coated hound often kept as a popular house pet today. The other three varieties are the BASSET BLEU DE GASCOGNE, a white dog with blue and black markings, and tan on the muzzle and feet; the BASSET FAUVE DE BRETAGNE, self-coloured and ranging from wheaten to deep red, with a short but hard coat; and finally the BASSET GRIFFON VENDEEN, a mainly white hound with markings of tan, black or grey on his unusual hard coat, typical of the Griffon breed.

Another small, short-legged hound breed is the Dachshund, which has spread from its native Germany to become extremely popular as a show dog and pet, all over the world. Some Dachshunds were given as gifts to Queen Victoria by Prince Edward of Saxe-Weimar-Eisenach, and one of these was exhibited in Birmingham during 1870. This small dog caused such interest that many other imports were soon made into Britain and the little hound quickly established itself. The breed, described as the German Badgerhound, gained Kennel Club recognition in 1874, and the British Dachshund Club, formed in 1881, has the distinction of being the oldest specialist canine breed club in the world.

The Dachshund was originally a smooth-coated dog with longer legs than his modern descendants, known as the Teckel in Germany. It is from the Teckel that the six modern varieties of Dachshund are derived, and it is thought that the long coats were the result of the introduction of Spaniel blood, while the wire-haired coats came from an infusion of Schnauzer. The original Teckel breed was used for several different types of hunting, sometimes as a scent hound, in packs, following fox or hare. Its purpose was, however, to hunt out animals that had gone to ground, and the hound had to be short enough to enter the earth or sett, fearless, and strong enough to attack.

Three miniature Long-haired Dachshund puppies awaiting their new owners.

Even the smallest of the Dachshunds makes a good guard and may be safely left in charge of property for short periods. Below, an alert miniature Wire-haired guards its owner's van.

The SMOOTH-HAIRED DACHSHUND is sporting and affectionate, always cheerful, and a very good watchdog. He is very easy to keep and needs very little food to keep his muscular body trim and in good condition. The short fine coat is rubbed over with a hound glove to produce a glow, and this variety may be of any solid colour, including red and chocolate. The Miniature Smooth-Haired Dachshund is a small replica of the standard but about half its weight, and it must not give any impression of being a 'toy' dog. The LONG-HAIRED DACHSHUND is of similar conformation, having a long and conical skull, long well-muscled body and a well-developed rib-cage. The legs are short but very strong and the feet are broad and quite large. The tail is long and undocked and is held out rather straight and not too high. Both the Long-haired and the Miniature Long-haired Dachshunds may be of any solid colour except white, and some are two coloured, as in the black and tan, or white and tan. The tan markings must be properly distributed according to the specific standard of points, and great attention is paid to the correct colour of the dog's nose and nails. Both long-haired varieties are very popular as pets and are very attractive, with silky feathering on the ears, tail chest and body.

The WIRE-HAIRED DACHSHUND, with its bushy eyebrows and bearded chin, has never quite achieved the popularity of the other varieties at shows but makes a hardy, healthy and happy house dog, being quiet indoors and possessing a charming, quizzical look.

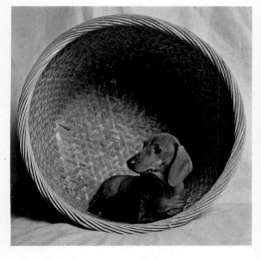

Above centre: A young puppy learning manners.
Above: A Smooth-haired Dachshund.

The ENGLISH FOXHOUND has a history dating back to the thirteenth century and was developed when foxhunting took over from staghunting as a fashionable contemporary pastime. Early packs had hounds of very mixed type and conformation, but the kennel system and keeping of stud records gradually produced a uniform type of hound. The Foxhound of today is probably the most efficient of all working animals, but being essentially a pack dog, he does not make a very good pet. Friendly, strong and built for stamina, allowing him to work all day and in all weather conditions, the Foxhound is large and rangy, and usually found in black, tan, white or lemon, or in any combination of these colours.

The AMERICAN FOXHOUND is longer in the leg and heavier than its English counterpart, from whom it is descended, the first breeding pairs having been taken to the Crown Colony by Robert Brooke in 1650, with further importations a century later. Four different functions are required of the American Foxhound, and so four slightly different varieties are found. The Field Trial events, run against the clock, need a hound that is long in the leg and very fast; the hunting of foxes with the gun requires a hound able to search out and find the quarry, and having a good voice with which to alert the hunters of its whereabouts; drag hunting, which is run over a prepared scent trail, needs a pack of fast, tough hounds, while normal pack hunting requires hounds with the same attributes as the English Foxhound – strength and endurance.

Left: A mature standard Wire-haired bitch.

Left: Foxhounds at the meet patiently waiting for the huntsman's signal to move off.

Below: These hounds hunt by scent and must work together as a coordinated pack.

An apprehensive trio
of young Basset
Hound pups.

Although the HARRIER looks rather like a small Foxhound, it is in fact a separate breed. The first pack of Harriers was founded in Britain in 1260 by Sir Elias of Midhope and was known as the Penistone pack. Although Xenophon is recorded as having used hounds for hare-hunting, in his day, about 400 B.C., nets were used into which the hares were driven before being killed for the table. Nets are never used in hunting the hare for sport, and hounds have been bred taller and fast enough to run it down. As with the Foxhound, there has been no attempt to establish the Harrier in the show ring in Britain; conversely there are more Harriers on the show bench in the United States than are found in the field. White with lemon, red, tan or black markings on his short, harsh coat, the Harrier is a tough and businesslike, medium sized hound with behaviour characteristic of the pack dog.

The BEAGLE was carefully bred to provide a hound suitable for small organizations and estates, where there were not sufficient resources to maintain large packs of big hounds. First developed in the sixteenth century from the smallest available Foxhounds and Harriers with the addition of Terrier blood, the general size of the breed was decreased without diminishing the scenting powers and courageous spirit of the hounds. Some strains of Beagle were bred smaller and smaller until a tiny hound known as the Pocket Beagle was produced, shown and hunted, then went out of favour. A rough-coated variety also appeared for a while, but again, this disappeared in favour of the smooth-coated standard variety. Although primarily a pack dog, the Beagle does make a fairly good pet, provided that he gets sufficient exercise and his owners understand his seemingly wilful attitude to life in general.

The BLACK AND TAN COONHOUND was only recognized by the American Kennel Club in 1945, although it is a very old breed, probably descended from the Talbot of Britain, through the Bloodhound and Foxhound. This hound will hunt normal game by scent, but was specifically bred for trailing raccoon and opossum, two nocturnal and climbing animals, and holding them at bay when finally treed, giving voice until joined by the huntsman who may then kill or spare the animals.

The BLOODHOUND is the oldest of all the scent hounds, being directly descended from the black St. Hubert Hounds, said to have been brought to Britain from the monastery at Ardennes, during the Norman invasion. Large and powerful and possessed of quite formidable scenting powers, this handsome, friendly dog is used more for trials than for showing.

Hickory is a perfect example of the family pet Beagle, loving, obedient and with a keen sense of fun.

Built mainly for speed, the hounds that hunt by sight have long legs and lithe, athletic bodies. Their necks are long, and the heads have forward-looking eyes with overlapping fields of view giving perfect vision. Of all hounds, the aristocratic AFGHAN has achieved the greatest rise in popularity since 1970. In its native land this dog was used as a guard at night, and to hunt deer and wolves. In other areas of the world it has become a glamorous show dog with a very long, silky coat which benefits from a good diet and lots of regular grooming.

The BORZOI, once known as the Russian Wolfhound, first appeared in the show rings of the world at the turn of this century. One of the swiftest of all dogs, the breed's Russian name is *Borzaja Sabaka* which means 'as fast as the wind'. Very like a greyhound in build, but taller and generally more powerful, the Borzoi has a long wavy coat, adding softness to its angular frame. Various colours are seen in this breed, but the most usual are white with fawn, brindle, red, blue or grey markings, offset with very dark, almond-shaped eyes.

The DEERHOUND was developed in Scotland for the purpose of keeping the large, indigenous herds of Red Deer under control by systematic culling. Acclaimed as a Scots native since the sixteenth century, and mentioned by Sir Walter Scott in many of his literary works, the imposing hound did his designated work willingly and efficiently. The modern Deerhound has changed very little over the years and is a very tall, rough-coated dog, having the typical build of the sight hound. A dark blue-grey is the most popular colour for the breed, although other acceptable colours include brindle and dark or light grey, also yellow, sandy-red or fawn with black mask and ears.

29

The GREYHOUND is one of the most ancient breeds and was used as a coursing hound by the Greeks and Romans. It was mentioned in the time of King Canute, and is still referred to in some regions by its old Saxon name *Greu* which means 'running dog'. In the sixteenth century the Greyhound was used for coursing buck, and King Henry VIII was said to be extremely fond of wagering on the times of his favourite hounds. Eventually, during the reign of Queen Elizabeth I, the Duke of Norfolk drew up rules for coursing, which remained in force for many years. Although the sport still takes place in some countries, the main role of the Greyhound has been transferred to the track, where since 1926 the sport of dog racing has attracted millions of fans.

Edendene Flicks of Druan is a Hamiltonstövare, otherwise known as the Swedish Foxhound.

The IRISH WOLFHOUND is the tallest of all dogs, and as its name implies, originated in Ireland centuries ago, where it was bred to accompany Celtic kings in the hunting of wolves and elk. Bewick wrote of the breed in 1792, remarking on its size and beauty, but by the early part of the nineteenth century, numbers had dwindled and the Wolfhound had almost died out. In 1860, due to the efforts of one Captain Graham, the breed was revived and eventually restored to its former glory, and the result is the wonderful wolfhound seen on the show bench today.

The SALUKI, one of the oldest members of the Greyhound family, is the coursing dog of the Bedouin, and like the Afghan hound was used mainly in conjunction with a hawk to hunt game in the desert. Often called the Gazelle hound, after the quarry it was trained to kill, the Saluki has always been a prized possession of the tribesmen of its homeland. Accepted in 1922 by the Kennel Club, the Saluki has become a superb show dog, gentle and dignified, with a friendly attitude towards humans. The smooth, soft coat with its attractive feather repays careful show preparation, and the athletic framework of the body needs adequate exercise to keep it in trim. There is a wide range of coat colours including white, cream, fawn, gold, red, grizzle and tan.

The WHIPPET is built like a small Greyhound and was first accepted by the Kennel Club in 1895, having been used for racing in the North of England for some time prior to this. Originally bred for catching rabbits, and coursing, the Whippet is a fine show dog, easy to prepare and handle, but it still takes part in races in some rural areas.

The RHODESIAN RIDGEBACK is thought to have been bred from the Cuban Bloodhound and the Hottentot Hunting Dog, from which it has inherited the characteristic ridge of hair along the spine which grows in the opposite direction to the rest of the coat. The breed was originally developed for tracking lions and bringing them to bay, resulting in a dog that was powerfully built, capable of a good turn of speed and completely fearless. It has a short, dense coat which is light to red wheaten in colour, sleek and glossy.

Two breeds of hound have the typically curled tails of the Spitz family. There is the smooth-coated, barkless BASENJI which originated in the Congo, and the rough-coated ELKHOUND, first bred in Scandinavia. The Basenji is an unusual hound with a permanently wrinkled brow, and sharply pricked ears on its flat-topped skull. It is a small but well-made dog, powerful for its size, and closely resembles the ringtailed dogs of the Ancient Egyptian tomb paintings. The Basenji was used by the Kiljongo natives of the Congo as pack hounds, to drive game into nets, and the dogs wore gourds, filled with pebbles, attached to their collars to make as much noise as possible. Eventually some of these attractive little dogs found their way into the show world, and have proved to make popular pets, although they love to fight with other dogs. The Basenji is either red, black or black and tan in colour and must have white feet, chest and tail tip according to the standard.

The Elkhound is a friendly and intelligent dog of medium size, but compactly and powerfully built. It was bred from Spitz ancestors for the express purpose of hunting the native deer of Scandinavia which is a formidable animal, the size of a horse, and with large, effective horns. In hunting the elk for food it was necessary to track the animal down through thick forests and tangled undergrowth, and one of the characteristics of the Elkhound is its coarse, thick and virtually indestructible coat, with an extra ruff protecting the throat.

The IBIZAN HOUND can lay claim to be the oldest breed in the world, for it completely resembles the hounds of the Pharaohs as depicted on tomb decorations, even down to the unusual pied markings. Having been bred true to type for five thousand years, this hound works by scent and sight, although the length of leg and general conformation point more to its primary function being a sight hound. It was first found on the Island of Ibiza in the Balearic group, and in the coastal regions of Majorca, Catalonia, Valencia and Provence, and was known as the PEDENGO, being used for hunting rabbits, hares and partridges. The Ibizan Hound males enjoy fighting one another, so when packs are used they consist of all bitches.

Uniquely, the Ibizan is able to work alone as well as in a pack, and is equally successful in hunting by night or by day. A true hound, it can be a little hard in temperament for showing, but repays care and quiet training. The rather disturbing eyes with their direct stare are of a pale clear amber and very expressive, and the coat may be white, chestnut or Lion solid colour, or in any combination of these colours.

Very similar to the Ibizan Hound, but slightly smaller in build and of a rich tan colour, the PHARAOH HOUND looks as though it has just stepped from the pages of the history books of three thousand years ago. For a considerable time, this hound was restricted to the island of Malta, which helped to keep it true to type, and although it was once considered to be merely a variation of the Ibizan Hound, it was finally accepted as a breed in its own right. Used as both a sight and scent hound, the body type indicates this dual purpose, and it has adapted to the role of show dog with great charm and panache. Friendly, clean and happy around the house, the Pharaoh Hound makes a good pet, but does need plenty of exercise to keep fit and well.

The final hound we shall discuss in this book is the rare and unusual OTTERHOUND, once very common and used in large packs to hunt the otter in Britain's lakes and rivers. Looking like a cross between a hound and a terrier, it has an unkempt, rough, hard coat and a woolly, waterproof undercoat which keeps it protected and dry during hunting.

Below: This gentle, grizzle-coloured Otterhound bitch is *Falconcrag Nymph.*

Bottom: The imposing Pharaoh Hound, a breed of great antiquity, represented by *Olio Amenophis of Edgeelmclere.*

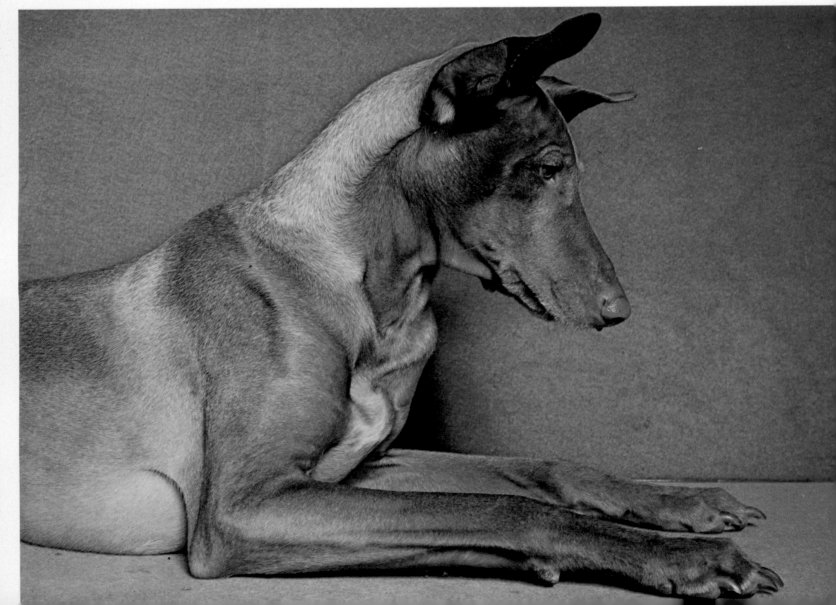

Working Dogs

An alert but kind family guard dog, Alsatian *Sheba of Huntingrove.*

The non-sporting group of working dogs may be loosely grouped into guard dogs, herding dogs and dogs developed mainly for draught work. In bygone days, no distinction was made between the dogs used for herding or as guards, for most of the animals were capable of both duties; even today many breeds perform dual roles in life.

The best of all guards, and the most popular pedigree dog in the world, is the ALSATIAN or GERMAN SHEPHERD DOG, which was developed for herding from the sheepdogs of Bavaria, and made its first appearance in the show ring in 1882. Highly intelligent and responsive to correct care and training, the Alsatian is greatly favoured for all types of police and military duties and makes an excellent guide dog for the blind. Other dogs with German origins are used in police work, including the PINSCHER, an old breed which is similar to a Manchester Terrier but has erect ears and a docked tail. In 1870 Herr Louis Dobermann crossed Pinschers with Rottweilers, and outcrossed the progeny with a herding dog and an English terrier, eventually producing the famed DOBERMANN PINSCHER, which was officially recognized in 1912. An elegant yet very muscular dog, it is fast and fearless, making a fine guard.

The ROTTWEILER itself is a well-established breed, more heavily built than its Dobermann descendants. This fiercely loyal guard dog gets its name from the small German market town of Rottweil, where it was first bred to drive cattle from the farms to market and to guard the drovers and their cash as they journeyed home again. Black, with some rich tan markings, the Rottweiler is intelligent and very easy to train.

The BOXER was developed in Germany around the year 1830, from crosses between a small Mastiff called the Bullenbeisser, and other breeds including the Bulldog, both of which were generally used in the then popular sport of bull-baiting. By 1895, the breed was ready for the show ring, and soon became established as one of the most popular of dogs. The Boxer is boisterous, friendly and very good with children, yet a sense of property makes it a good house dog and excellent guard.

Right: The elegant
black Groenendael is
Nirvana Adulation.

Right: A Bearded
Collie poses happily
for the photographer.

There are many dog breeds which were specially developed for their skill and aptitude in herding sheep. The COLLIE breeds are particularly well known in Britain, the name having been derived from that of the Colley, an agile and nervous breed of black-faced sheep once found in the Scottish Highlands. The dogs which tended them had to be extraordinarily clever in their work, and were called Scotch Colley Dogs. The ROUGH COLLIE is a glamorous dog, selectively bred for the show ring during the past few decades, causing the length of the head to become somewhat exaggerated and the profuse coat to take on a softer quality. The three recognized colours are sable and white, tri-colour and blue merle, and a good specimen is a very attractive dog. The SMOOTH COLLIE is much rarer than the Rough Collie, although the two breeds are virtually identical except for coat length, and are found in the same colours.

The BEARDED COLLIE is a very different animal, although it also had its origins in Scotland. The coat is quite harsh, long and shaggy, and the head is square with a blunt muzzle. Temperamentally, this is a delightful breed, and its soft nature makes it more suitable for driving cattle than herding sheep. Nevertheless, Bearded Collies are still used as working dogs, and are also very popular in the show ring, often being handled by quite young children.

The OLD ENGLISH SHEEPDOG probably shares a common ancestry with the Bearded Collie, and a similar dog is shown in the Gainsborough portrait of the Third Duke of Buccleuch, painted in 1771. Found in any shade of grizzle, grey, blue or blue merle, with or without white markings, the long coat of this breed is profuse and has a waterproof undercoat. Playful and boisterous when young, the Old English has a delightful temperament and makes a fine guard, being especially good with children. The SHETLAND SHEEPDOG is built rather like a miniature Rough Collie, but has distinct differences in the shape of the head. A working breed, this small dog was developed in the Shetland Isles, renowned also for the small size of their sheep and their diminutive Shetland ponies.

Closely related to the Alsatian, and having the same basic body shape, are three sheepdog breeds from Belgium. The GROENENDAEL, which has a long black coat, comes from a village of the same name, near Brussels. Bred first as a herding dog, the breed gained recognition as a guard and efficient messenger in the First World War, and later found a niche in police work in the United States. The MALINOIS is of similar conformation but has a short thick coat of dark fawn with a black overlay, muzzle and ears. It excels in all herding and guard duties. The TERVUEREN is a warm, mahogany colour with a black overlay and black tipping to the face, ears and tail. Looking very like a rough-coated Alsatian, this dog is very intelligent and trains to any duties.

The BRIARD is an ancient French breed, taking its name from the province of Brie. It was used as a guard as well as a herding dog during the nineteenth century when the flocks were prone to attack by wolves. Still used extensively as a sheepdog in France, this long-coated dog may be of any solid colour, but is generally seen in black or slate grey. Another dog which is gaining popularity is the BOUVIER DES FLANDRES from south-western Flanders and northern France. Its name means 'cowherd' and indicates the breed's original purpose. The Bouvier des Flandres is primarily a working animal, but has also caught the imagination in the show ring, being large and impressive with an alert and interested air. It is easy to train and responsive, and very loyal to family and friends. Rough, tousled and unkempt-looking, this breed's coat is very hardy and may be fawn to black, pepper and salt, grey or brindle.

Two breeds of Hungarian sheep dogs have strange corded coats which need special attention when the animals are kept as pets or show dogs. The KOMONDOR is one of these dogs and the breed dates back to 1555, since when it has remained virtually unchanged. The Racka sheep of the ancient Magyar tribes are said to have had coats similar to that of the Komondor, which proved to be the perfect herding dog for the large intractable animals. Later, when herds of smaller, more docile sheep were introduced, the Komondor assumed the role of guardian, while the smaller, and darker but similarly built PULI took over the herding duties. The Komondor is always white in colour while the Puli may be black, rusty black or various shades of grey and white. Both breeds need special care for showing, for the unusual coat must have the cords carefully parted at the age of six months and attended to regularly, so that the long twists remain unmatted. These dogs cannot be brushed and are never combed. After bathing, the coat is carefully separated and the cords encouraged to hang in long strips.

Javiltreva Bodros, a Komondor dog shows his typically corded coat.

Right: Two Komondor exhibits, with their proud owner, wait patiently on their bench before their class is called at Cruft's Dog Show, London.

Far right: Beautiful slate-and-white Bearded Collie *Pebhallows Puddle Jumper*.

Looking somewhat bored on his show bench, a melancholy Maremma sheepdog waits his turn in the ring.

A rather immature but well-behaved Maremma sheepdog, *Cyrano Oriano*.

One of the largest of the herding dogs is the MAREMMA sheepdog, an ancient breed believed to have descended from the white dogs of the Magyars, for dogs of this type have been depicted in paintings for many years. The breed takes its name from the fertile coastal plains of Maremma, north of Rome, Italy, where it was used for guarding and driving the flocks and herds to and from the mountains to graze. The KUVASZ is another, similar, large white dog, developed primarily as a guard, although it proved its worth also in herding. It was also kept in packs for hunting by the Hungarian Royal Family during the fifteenth century, and the king kept a Kuvasz as his personal guard. The PYRENEAN MOUNTAIN DOG, also white, is slightly larger than the Maremma and the Kuvasz and its head shows the influence of its Tibetan Mastiff ancestors. It was first developed to guard flocks of sheep against marauding wolves and bears in the Pyrenees, and later, wearing a spiked iron collar, became a dog of war. Today he is still used as a guide and pack animal, as well as being a noble-looking show dog.

The MASTIFF has obscure origins, but dogs of this type are clearly shown on Ancient Egyptian friezes and tomb paintings, and were used by the Romans as war dogs. The Roman armies had an officer called the Procurator of Dogs stationed in Britain, whose task it was to select Mastiffs for transportation to the amphitheatres in Rome for the sport of bear-baiting. In medieval times the Mastiff was a popular guard dog, and often accompanied its master into battle. Today this massive dog is fairly rare, and does not enjoy being a showman. It makes a supreme guard, being fiercely protective of its property and human family. The Mastiff is easy to keep in good condition, given an adequate, well-balanced diet. The short, close-lying coat may be apricot, silver, fawn or brindle, with a black muzzle, ears and nose.

The BULL MASTIFF is the result of crossing the Mastiff with other breeds including the Bulldog. It was first recognized in 1924, and was greatly appreciated for its guarding potential. Another of the Mastiff group is the majestic GREAT DANE, originally a fighting dog, then bred lighter for use in hunting wild boar in the seventeenth century. It makes a superb show dog, and despite its size is a perfect pet. The ST. BERNARD is descended from the Alpine Mastiff, and is reputed to have been kept by the monks of the Hospice of Saint Bernard for over three hundred years, and used to rescue snowbound travellers in the Swiss Alps. A strong dog and one of the heaviest of all breeds, it is not easy to keep, needing lots of space, plenty of food and adequate exercise, but the St. Bernard does make a magnificent and rewarding show dog.

Above: The family dog is happy to take his place in the parade at the Brawley Cattle Call Rodeo in California, U.S.A.

Left: *Sacul Oonar*, a grey-brindle Bouvier des Flandres.

Using dogs for haulage work is illegal in Britain, but sturdy breeds were used to pull delivery carts in Europe until quite recent times. The most popular of these dogs were the LEONBERGER and the BERNESE MOUNTAIN DOG. Today the only dogs regularly used for heavy draught work are sled dogs, generally used in teams for pulling sledges on long journeys over land covered with snow and ice. The common name for all varieties of sled dog is the Husky, but only one of the four recognized varieties of northern draught dogs to which it should apply is the SIBERIAN HUSKY. This dog was known as the Chukchi, after the north-east Asian tribe with which it was associated, and maintained by them as a pure breed, being highly valued for its strength, speed and powers of endurance. An impressive dog of medium size and with a double coat, the Siberian Husky is friendly and makes a good pet.

The ALASKAN MALAMUTE is one of the oldest of the sled breeds and is named after the Malemute tribe of Alaska. Famous for its powers of endurance, the Malamute was used in the famous arctic explorations of the past, and is now employed in the competitive sport of sled racing. In the long-distance races, teams of six dogs pull a load weighing some 600 lb, for an average of 50 miles a day, for several days. This dog has retained many of the features of the Spitz family from which it has descended, including the characteristically curled tail, held up and over the back. The small, erect and triangular ears, perfect for cold weather conditions, are another Spitz feature, as is the very short dense, coarse coat, and the ruff protecting the neck.

Embodying true Husky type, the ESKIMO DOG is part of the heritage of northern Canada. Known to the Innuit as the 'Kingmik' it originated in Greenland, and for many years provided the only form of transport in the remote and inhospitable regions of that land. A large, strong dog, with a weatherproof coat, it is often found with most attractive markings, and has begun to find favour around the world as a show dog The SAMOYED is the last of the four sled dogs. Another Spitz type, it originated in Siberia among the nomadic Samoyed tribe and was useful in herding their caribou, as well as hauling sledges. Originally black, or with tan or white markings in its native land, the thick double coat of the Samoyed of the show ring is glistening white, white and cream, or cream, and is virtually weatherproof. The dog has a kind expression, with beautiful dark brown, almond-shaped eyes, outlined with black, matching its lips and nose-leather.

Left: *Ardfauld Canticle* is a red wheaten bitch of the rare Spitz breed known as the Norwegian Buhund.

Above: A protective Siberian Husky on the show bench with two young friends.

Some dogs are associated with the herding of cattle rather than sheep and the most famous of these are the two WELSH CORGI breeds, the Cardigan and the Pembroke. For hundreds of years these short-legged dogs drove cattle from the hills and valleys of Wales to the Smithfield cattle market in London. They were trained to nip at the heels of the cattle in order to keep them moving steadily, and were known colloquially as 'heelers'. Both varieties of Corgi are similar in build, but the Cardigan is slightly longer in the body and heavier than its more popular relative. It is also allowed to retain its full and rather bushy tail, whereas the Pembroke (right) has its tail docked short. Both of the Corgi breeds make excellent pet and show dogs, if kept trim with the correct diet and exercise, and are also good guards. The Cardigan has a short to medium length, hard coat which may be of any colour except pure white, while the Pembroke may be found in self-coloured red, sable, fawn, black and tan, or with the addition of white markings on the legs, chest and neck. Some white is allowed on the head or muzzle, but any piebald or skewbald effect, or any hound-like markings are considered faults in the breed. Very similar to the Corgi but with dull coat colours of grey, brownish yellow or brindle, the SWEDISH VALHUND is a friendly, active pet and guard.

Considered to be the most important breed of dog in Japan, the AKITA was originally used for hunting boar and deer. A typical Spitz with wedge-shaped skull, stiff fur and a curled and bushy tail, this dog is now mainly used as a house dog and pet, and is especially good with children. Double coated, the Akita may be of any colour including brindle, with or without a mask or blaze. The small, deep-set eyes are dark brown with black rims, and the ears are triangular and pricked. Another breed of the Spitz type is the NORWEGIAN BUHUND, included in the Working Group in most countries. It has the short body, pricked ears, curled tail and stand-off coat common to the Spitz family. First bred as a general farm and guard dog, the Buhund has proved to have good herding capabilities. Sharp yet friendly, it is intelligent and has great powers of endurance. A small dog, the Buhund is well balanced and firm muscled, and the double, weatherproof coat may be wheaten, black, light to medium red, or wolf-sable in colour. Black masks and ears are permitted, as well as small, symmetrical white markings on the chest, legs, blaze and neck.

In Australia there is a manufactured herding dog which resembles a small Alsatian, and is said to have been derived from crossing the Collie with the Dingo. The resulting breed is called the AUSTRALIAN CATTLE DOG, previously called the Australian Heeler, having a habit similar to that of the Welsh Corgi of nipping at the heels of the cattle to drive them on. A previous Australian breed, the Black Bobtail, had proved unable to withstand the heat and strain of cattle driving, but with the Dingo and Collie outcrosses and some Dalmatian, an efficient breed emerged.

A Shetland sheepdog puppy at six weeks of age.

Although not officially recognized as a breed, the Border Collie seems to be fairly consistent in type and is very popular for obedience work. Right: A Border Collie bitch. Below: *Corrie of Houndean* demonstrates the High Jump technique.

Above: The British prison services prefer to use expertly trained German Shepherd dogs for guard duties.

The BORDER COLLIE and the WELSH COLLIE are two closely related breeds not recognized by the Kennel Club, being bred for their performance and aptitude for work, rather than for their strict adherence to a standard of show points for appearance. The success of such breeding has been proven by the fact that these two working collie breeds have ousted the national breeds such as the Rough Collie, and perform the majority of the herding work in Britain today. These working collies are of medium size and generally black with symmetrical white markings. Highly intelligent and with an in-built desire to please, the collies thrive on long and rigorous training routines. They make wonderful dogs for competitions such as sheepdog trials, and the very demanding tests of obedience, staged at the major dog shows.

The Obedience Championship classes at London's annual Cruft's Dog Show has many entrants each year, all of whom have qualified by having won a Kennel Club Obedience Certificate. Seven tests are given, and the handler may only give one command or signal, except in the second test, where two are allowed. The first test is for Heel Work and requires the dog to walk freely at heel, at fast and slow paces and to be left at 'stand', 'sit' and 'down'. The second test requires the dog to be sent away, to drop when told and to recall instantly. Test three is a simple retrieving exercise, while test four calls for control from a distance, with the dog assuming various positions on commands given in random order. The fifth test requires the dog to sit and remain unmoving for two minutes while its handler is out of sight, while the sixth test is even more demanding, for the dog must stay in the 'down' position for ten minutes, again with the handler out of sight. Finally the seventh test requires the dog to be given the scent of the judge, then to select a cloth impregnated by the same scent from a selection of cloths placed about the arena.

There are few sights more exciting than watching the finalists in an obedience trial competing for top honours. The dogs seem to revel in their work, are eager to get on with the job and delighted when they perform correctly. The most successful candidates in such contests are the Working and Border Collies, some crossbred sheepdogs and Alsatians or German Shepherd Dogs.

Terriers

Right: The Australian Silky Terrier is really a Toy Dog, having been bred to a diminutive size.

Right: A Wire Fox Terrier with her young daughter.

The group of dogs known as Terriers gets its name from *terra*, the Latin word for earth, for they were chiefly bred for the destruction of vermin, many of which had to be dug out of their underground holes, dens and burrows. Most of today's Terrier breeds originated in Britain, some basic stock having been clearly recorded as long ago as the fifteenth century, and by the year 1677 they had been divided into two distinct groups. The first of these was described as being short-haired and crooked-legged, perfect for working underground; the second type, longer in the leg, with a shaggy, weather-resistant coat was more suited to hunting above ground, but was also prepared to dig furiously for its quarry if gone to earth.

Terriers were selectively bred, and the various country regions of Britain took a pride in their own type of dogs. The earliest recognized variety in this group was the Old English White Terrier, which is now extinct. It was a smooth-coated, white dog, rather like a cross between a Bull Terrier and a Smooth Fox Terrier, fierce, aggressive and strong. Working men liked the weekend sport of ratting in and around the big industrial plants that sprang up in the north and west of the country, and developed small sharp terriers for the purpose. Some medium sized dogs were bred with slightly longer legs, and were used for working with packs of Foxhounds. When a fox was run to earth, the hunt terriers could follow it down and either drive the animal from its hiding place or hold it at bay until the huntsmen could dig it out.

Dogs with strong jaws and powerful bodies combined with rather short legs, such as the Sealyham and Dandie Dinmont, were used as badger hounds, for the badger can be a formidable adversary when cornered, and a strong and fearless dog was needed to dispatch him. The natural tenacity of the Terrier was taken into account when fighting dogs were required, and the best of these were bred from Terriers crossed with Bulldogs. Eventually, dog-fighting became illegal, badgers were protected, and the species of hunted animals dramatically declined, causing many Terriers to become redundant. Luckily for them, however, their reputations and convenient sizes ensured their survival as pets, and for an occasional day's sport if they are country dogs. They have also prospered as show dogs, each type being carefully bred to its exacting standard.

The largest of the Terrier group is the AIREDALE, which is often called the 'King of Terriers', not only for his size, but because he embodies all of the Terrier features. A well established breed, he was originally bred and used in packs for otterhunting in the lovely valleys of the Wharfe and Aire in South Yorkshire, and it is from the Aire Valley that he got his name, when the breed was accepted in 1878. Previously known as the Waterside or Bingley Terrier, he was much more hound-like than he is today, and probably was produced by crossing Otterhounds with small black and tan ratting terriers. Selective breeding soon reduced his large ears, squared up his conformation and standardized his coat, so that the dog of today is very distinctive indeed. The body is black or dark grizzle, the head and lower legs are tan, and the ears are of a darker tan shade. The coat itself is very special, being hard, dense and wiry and just very slightly waved. The Airedale is a very loyal and protective dog and so makes a really excellent guard. It is also extremely versatile, being used in police work and as an efficient messenger during the First World War. Today it is best known as a smart and successful show dog, although the coat requires a considerable amount of shaping and careful trimming.

The AUSTRALIAN TERRIER was first shown in Melbourne in 1872, when it was called the Broken-Coated Terrier. Later it became the Blue and Tan, then the Toy and underwent many name changes until it received Kennel Club status in Britain in 1933. This little dog is one of the smallest of the working Terriers, but carries out his duties with such an air of importance that he often seems to be a much larger dog. He makes a very good pet and a fine watchdog, having acute powers of sight and hearing, and is excellent with children. As a show dog the Australian Terrier needs very little preparation, for the coat is straight and hard and kept in good condition by correct diet and regular grooming. Looking very similar to the Yorkshire Terrier in general conformation, the main variety has a blue or silver-grey body with rich tan on the face and legs and a blue or silver-grey top-knot. The second variety, possibly introduced by out-crossing the original blue and tan dogs with Cairn Terriers, is rarer, and a clear sandy-red with matching top-knot.

The AUSTRALIAN SILKY TERRIER belongs in the Toy Group, but was bred alongside the Australian Terrier for some years, and in fact shared its breed club. It is like a Yorkshire Terrier in shape and size, but with a shorter and very silky coat, which breeders prefer to be of a really rich dark blue, with tan on the legs and feet. Decorative and handsome, he has more of the Terrier in him than the Toy, and much prefers to be actively engaged than sitting in his basket.

When trimmed correctly for the show ring, the BEDLINGTON TERRIER

Champion Dalip Huggy Bear, a famous and very beautiful, blue Bedlington Terrier dog.

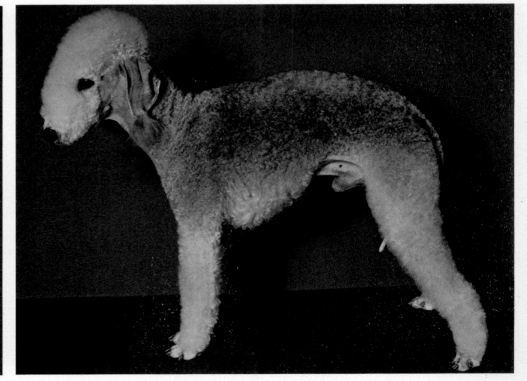

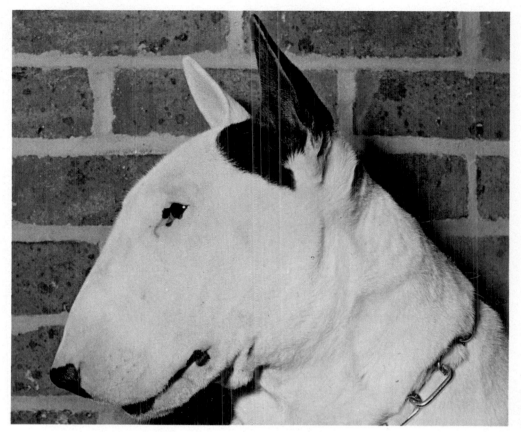

The Bull Terrier makes a fearless and often very fierce guard dog.

looks rather like a little lamb, having a very distinctive coat with the appearance of lamb's wool, especially on the legs and top-knot. This coat may be blue, blue and tan, liver or sandy in colour, and darker pigments are most encouraged. The glamorous little dog is far from lamb-like in its sporting activities, for it is very fast and extremely agile, and makes an ideal Terrier for ratting or rabbiting. Originally known as the Rothbury Terrier, the breed was given its present name in 1825 by a mason called Joseph Aynsley, and was probably bred from the Whippet and the Dandie Dinmont Terriers. It does look rather like a Whippet in build, with the addition of the woolly coat.

One of the older breeds of Terrier is the DANDIE DINMONT. It first appeared about 1700 when it was used for hunting badger, fox and otter in the border counties of England. It did not get its present name, however, until 1814, when a character in Sir Walter Scott's novel *Guy Mannering*, called Dandie Dinmont, owned a pack of these sporting dogs. The novel aroused such interest in the breed that it seemed natural to name it after the book's character. Dandie Dinmonts are mustard or pepper in colour with lighter points and top-knots.

Originally bred for fighting and for ratting contests, the BULL TERRIER is descended from the Old English White Terrier and the Bulldog, with the possible addition of one or two other breeds to add their particular features and traits. By 1860, a pure white strain of Bull Terriers had been raised and when shown, swept the board. These first show dogs had heads with distinct stops and quite bold eyes, but selective breeding has produced the oval head and oblique narrow eyes so typical of the breed today. Still preferred in pure white, dogs are not penalized in the ring for showing dark head markings, and coloured dogs, preferably brindles, are allowed in Britain but are classed as a separate breed variety in the United States. Being totally fearless, the Bull Terrier makes a magnificent guard and takes a possessive pride in its family and home. It is a very affectionate dog and seems to have a particular rapport with children.

The MINIATURE BULL TERRIER is a perfect small replica of the standard, while the STAFFORDSHIRE BULL TERRIER was bred more like the Bulldog, and especially for fighting in the pits, often to the death, until the sport was eventually banned. It still has the inherent tendency to scrap with other dogs, but is affectionate and friendly towards humans.

Salismore Minting, a
mustard Dandie
Dinmont Terrier.

The SMOOTH FOX TERRIER has retained a constant level of popularity over the years and dates back to the Old English Terrier of the fifteenth century. The dog as we know it today can be traced back directly to 1860, and in 1862 one of these dogs, called 'Old Jock', was first shown in Birmingham. The standard of points drawn up by the Fox Terrier Club in those early days has changed very little, but the Fox Terrier of today has grown too tall and refined to be of much use in the field going to ground after a fox, as his ancestors would have done. The WIRE FOX TERRIER is closely related to the smooth variety, and came from the same half-coated root stock. This breed must be regularly trimmed to keep the wiry coat manageable. Both Fox Terriers make affectionate and loyal pets. They are very distrustful of strangers however, and so make very good guard dogs.

The LAKELAND TERRIER was produced in the strong hunting region of the English Lake District when some of the local strains of terriers such as the Patterdale, the Elterwater and the Fell Terrier were intermated, and the Lakeland Terrier was recognized as a breed in 1921. First used extensively with the hunt, this small compact dog is now renowned as a superb show dog, as well as a neat and tidy house pet.

The WELSH TERRIER is sometimes confused with the Lakeland, as both breeds may be found in black and tan, and both have the same sort of harsh and wiry coat. The breeds look quite different, however, when seen side by side, the heads being totally dissimilar. The Welsh Terrier was called Ynysfor during the eighteenth century, and ran with foxhounds in the hills of North Wales.

The IRISH TERRIER is a handsome dog and very distinctive, being wheaten to bright red in colour, which has given rise to his affectionate nick-name of the 'Red Devil'. The glowing coat must be trimmed for showing, to display the dog's long, lithe lines. Another Irish breed is the remarkable KERRY BLUE TERRIER, first bred in the area known as the Ring of Kerry. This Terrier is thought to have been developed from the Gadhar, an extinct sheepdog of Ireland, with some Greyhound and Setter blood. Although typically Terrier in many respects, and always ready to stand up for himself in a fight, the Kerry Blue also makes an efficient gundog. The puppies of this breed are born pure black and only slowly develop their blue coats.

Halisblu Stylist, a carefully trimmed Kerry Blue Terrier.

Above: A red Lakeland Terrier, handsome *Louieville Red Baron*.

Right: Fox Terrier pups.

Champion
Burrowdown
Heatwave, a superb
black-and-tan
Manchester Terrier
dog.

Least known and most unusual of the three native Terriers of Ireland is the SOFT-COATED WHEATEN TERRIER. This rare dog is known to have existed for many years and the breed has remained constant in type and conformation for the last century. Developed as a general purpose dog for use on farms and smallholdings, the Wheaten had to guard property and deal with the dispatch of vermin to earn his keep. This dog has a soft, silky coat the colour of ripening wheat, and it should be left as natural as possible, even for the show ring. Very obedient and easy to train, this breed makes an ideal, fun-loving pet.

The MANCHESTER TERRIER is a no-nonsense sort of dog of the type which has existed in Britain for centuries. It has a close, smooth and glossy coat, firm in texture and jet black in colour with rich mahogany tan markings on the muzzle, the cheeks, above each eye and on the lower legs. This colour distribution is similar to the pattern found on the Dobermann and Rottweiler breeds, and records of the old Black and Tan Terrier of Britain show that it was marked in exactly the same way. The Black and Tan was renowned for its ability to kill rats, and contests were arranged in which the dogs were released into pits with a hundred rats, then timed while they dispatched them all. A Terrier called 'Billy' is said to have held the record time of 6½ minutes for completing the job.

The Black and Tan was crossed with the Whippet to produce the first Manchester Terriers, which had a rather chequered career before finally finding a niche in the show world, and a place in the home as an easily cared for pet.

Above: *And Harry of Titanium*, a big name for a small but game Norfolk Terrier.

Above right: Terrier puppies like this young Yorkie are usually bold and adventurous, and though quite precocious are easy to train.

Above: The very attractive and unusual Soft Coated Wheaten Terrier.

The BORDER TERRIER acquired his name from his association with the Border Hunt, whose Master carefully bred his Terriers for efficiency in their work with the foxhound pack. The ideal Terrier had to be fairly long in the leg to enable him to keep up with hounds, and he had to be small enough to go to ground after a fox. Added to this, a certain amount of strength and courage was required to cope with the situation in which he might find himself underground, unable to reverse and face to face with a frightened and dangerous animal at bay. Through trial and error, and a great deal of perseverance, the early breeders did in fact manage to produce just such a Terrier, and the Border Terrier Club was formed for its protection in 1921. The breed has become popular as pets in recent years and is making a mark in shows. This very businesslike little dog has a harsh topcoat and a soft undercoat. He is red, wheaten, grizzle and tan, or blue and tan in colour, without white, except on the chest.

Two very similar breeds of Terrier were established in East Anglia, both with harsh, wiry coats, and found in similar colours of either red, wheaten, black and tan or grizzle, and without any white markings. The first to be established was the NORWICH TERRIER, which was accepted by the Kennel Club as a recognized breed in 1932. At that time there was only the one Terrier of Norfolk, which had either upright or drooping ears. First used in the middle of the nineteenth century for hunting fox and badger, this little dog became the favourite of the students of nearby Cambridge University, who would go vermin hunting during their free periods, and needed a very unobtrusive breed of dog to keep in their rooms. The Norwich Terrier of today is distinguished by erect and well set ears with pointed tips. The NORFOLK TERRIER is so like the Norwich Terrier that the layman would be hard pressed to tell them apart. It does have a smoother muzzle however, and quite different ears which drop towards the cheeks. Both breeds are alike in habits and disposition, and they make ideal family pets, being loving, easy to train and very obedient.

The SEALYHAM TERRIER was first bred in Wales by John Edwards, an eccentric who lived on the Sealyham estate in Pembrokeshire and wanted his own strain of Terriers for hunting. His foundation stock was picked from dogs which showed the best rat-catching traits, regardless of their looks, colour or conformation, and his first pack was a mixed and motley collection of Terriers. Eventually, with the introduction of the Dandie Dinmont and Bull Terrier, the breed slowly developed its present characteristics, and has achieved an acceptable level of popularity today, both in the show ring and as a quite captivating pet. An attractive little dog, long in the body, short-legged and with a quite distinctive head, the Sealyham is generally white in colour, or white with lemon, brown or badger pied markings on the head and ears.

One of the oldest of the Terrier breeds is the CAIRN which originated on the Island of Skye. Essentially a working dog, this Terrier was used to work among rocky crags and fells, to bolt foxes, badgers and otters, and it

This little West Highland White Terrier is *Cedarfell Masterfull*.

Overleaf: *Fenbeach Venus*, a Skye Terrier.

is from its skill in the cairns that it derived its name. A gay little dog, the Cairn has a double, weather-resistant coat which may be red, sandy, grey, brindled or nearly black. The SCOTTISH TERRIER was also first developed on the Island of Skye, but became known as the Aberdeen Terrier, and was generally black in colour. The Scottish Terrier Club was formed in 1882 and the standards of perfection for the breed drawn up at that time have changed very little. The most striking feature of the breed is the distinctive head, with its square, well furnished muzzle, long skull and bushy eyebrows. It may be wheaten or of any brindled colour as well as black, and the double coat is completely weatherproof. The 'Scottie' may be a little sharp, having a true Terrier temperament, but is good with its own family and friends.

The third Terrier to have been developed on the Island of Skye, is in fact called the SKYE TERRIER. A low-slung dog with a long and glamorous coat, its looks belie its character for it is an excellent hunter, game and courageous, and an awe-inspiring fighter, always ready for a scrap with other dogs. This breed is thought to have been used in the development of the Yorkshire Terrier in Britain and the Australian Silky. The Skye makes a good show dog, for the coat is fairly simple to prepare, and a regular routine grooming keeps it in immaculate order. Found in several solid colours, the ears and nose of the Skye Terrier must always be black.

The WEST HIGHLAND WHITE was first known as the Poltalloch Terrier, and has always been an all-white breed. It was originally bred for hunting foxes in very rocky terrain, and the dog had to be strong and brave enough to force its way through rock crevices and narrow openings in pursuit of its quarry. An amusing companion and a perfect house dog, the 'Westie', as it is affectionately known, is a happy, cheeky little dog, with dark, intelligent eyes and alertly pricked ears.

The Utility Group

The Utility Group consists of a very mixed assortment of non-sporting breeds and includes a number of national dogs, such as America's Boston Terrier, Britain's Bulldog, the French Poodle and the Chinese Chow Chow. A Utility class at a top dog show is very interesting, too, because all the dogs are of different shapes, sizes and colours, they move with different actions, have quite different standards of show points and were bred for quite different purposes.

The CHOW CHOW has existed in China for at least two hundred years and was originally bred for its skin and for meat. A massive, heavy-boned dog of medium height, the Chow Chow is a typical prick-eared, curled-tail Spitz with a profuse coat, generally black, red, blue, fawn, cream or white, sometimes shaded, but never parti-coloured. Chows are quite delightful as puppies, looking just like cuddly teddy bears. They are rather aloof at times, however, and can be very difficult to train, though quite well behaved when they feel so inclined.

Another Spitz in this group is the KEESHOND, the barge-dog from Holland, a small, wolf-grey animal that makes an excellent pet and a good guard. Although he is fairly large, he can curl up small, head and tail tucked tightly in, just as his Husky cousins curl up in Arctic snow.

The barge-dog of Belgium is the SCHIPPERKE, and is yet another small Spitz. This one's name comes from a corruption of the word for 'little skipper', referring to his imperious attitude aboard his barge home. Like many of the Spitz family, the Schipperke is very much a one-man dog, a fact that is particularly apparent in the show ring, when it will stand and attend its handler, totally oblivious of all that is going on around. Originally allowed only in black, other whole colours such as cream and fawn appeared in litters from time to time and were eventually accepted in the breed's standard.

A Boston Terrier puppy is usually extrovert and can be an amusing and easily cared-for pet.

A Champion Boston Terrier, *Balleris Johnny Go Lightly*.

Donna Dale Miss Rose Bud, a fawn French Bulldog.

The DALMATIAN is a very interesting dog, quite large and strongly built, with a short, sparkling-white coat dotted with large and quite distinct black or liver spots. It was fashionable in the nineteenth century to have a Dalmatian trotting along between the wheels under the carriage. Its role was that of guard, and in the case of an attack it was expected to leap out and put the assailant to flight. Said to have originated in Dalmatia, this dog was probably bred from spotted or harlequin Great Danes, crossed with Pointers to reduce and compact its size and to improve the markings. Very intelligent and usually well behaved, the Dalmatian is well established as a house dog.

In many countries the BOSTON TERRIER is thought of as the national dog of America, although the breed originated from a cross between a Bulldog and an English Terrier, and was later improved by the careful introduction of some French Bulldog blood. Officially recognized in 1893 when they were given their present name, it is possible that some of the early Boston Terriers were encouraged to fight for sport. This dapper little short-coated dog should be brindle in colour with quite distinctive white markings, but black with white is allowed.

The FRENCH BULLDOG is smaller and more energetic than his British counterpart and is easily distinguished by his large 'bat' ears. It is held that this breed is descended from the Dogue of Bordeaux, a large mastiff type, but it is more probable that it is the result of selective breeding from very small Bulldogs. The French Bulldog is an excellent family pet and is active and amusing, taking a great interest in all that goes on. He does not bark but communicates by making an unusual and distinctive guttural sound deep in his throat.

The BULLDOG was bred from the Mastiff, and by a process of careful and selective breeding, the legs were gradually reduced in length. This was done in order to produce a dog suitable for the sport of bull-baiting, very popular in Britain until it was made illegal in 1835. The bull would be tied to a stake in an open space, and the Bulldogs were set to 'pin' the enraged animal by the nose. Dogs were tossed constantly but attacked time and time again until the bull was worn down and finally pinned, and large sums of money were wagered on the dogs' performances. When bull-baiting was banned, the Bulldog was bred as a fighting dog, but proved less fit for this purpose than the Bull Terrier. Eventually the Bulldog Club Incorporated was formed in 1864 to protect the breed. The Bulldog must be kept fit in order to look his best, and must never be allowed to become overweight. The breed standard describes his colour as being whole or smut, which is whole coloured with the addition of a black mask or muzzle.

A family group of Bulldogs.

The GIANT SCHNAUZER only recently started its show career outside its native Germany. It is possible that this dog was developed from breeds such as the Bouvier des Flandres and the Briard, which are similar in colour and have the same squarely built body. The origin of his hard, wiry coat however, remains rather obscure. This coat needs quite a lot of show preparation, although it looks quite acceptable when left rough. Very like an Airedale Terrier about the head, the breed is more reliable than the Terriers in temperament but needs careful training to produce an acceptably disciplined dog. A smaller version of the breed is the SCHNAUZER, powerfully built, and an active and very effective guard for a small home or large factory. The MINIATURE SCHNAUZER is a really trim little fellow conforming to the same basic standard as the larger versions of the breed. He is very squarely built and is trimmed to exaggerate this effect. He is a game little dog and likes nothing better than the opportunity to hunt; nevertheless his neat size and clean habits make him the ideal dog for life in a small town home.

All the Schnauzers have dark, oval eyes, set well forward and hooded by arched, bushy eyebrows. The neat and V-shaped ears are set high, dropping forward at the temples and adding to the slightly quizzical expression of the breed. The coat colour is important and may be pure black, or all pepper and salt colours in even proportions.

Perhaps the best known, and by far the most popular breed in the Utility Group is the POODLE, which is especially suitable for town life and will live quite happily in a flat or apartment. The breed has the advantage of a coat that never moults and does not harbour any vestige of doggy odours. It does need regular trimming, however, and a daily routine brushing to keep the coat in good order.

There are three sizes in the Poodle family, the STANDARD POODLE which is quite a large and substantial dog, the small MINIATURE POODLE and the tiny TOY POODLE.

The Standard Poodle was almost certainly bred originally as a large gundog, known as the Water Dog or Pudel of Germany. Later he found his way to the rings of the French circus as he was intelligent and agile enough to perform difficult tricks with great ease. Originally shown with a corded coat, as seen in the Puli and the Komondor today, modern poodles are clipped for the show ring in a variety of accepted styles. In Britain the Kennel Club prefers the traditional Lion clip, while the American Kennel Club states that the poodle may be shown in the Puppy, English Saddle (Lion) clip, or the traditional Continental clip, and that poodles shown in any other clip shall be disqualified. Poodles under one year old may be shown in Puppy clip with the coat left long and the face, throat, feet and base of the tail shaved. The entire shaven foot has to be visible and there must be a pompom on the end of the shaven tail.

The Miniature Poodle is probably nearer to the size of the original Pudel, the Standard having been selectively bred for its larger size, and the Toy bred for its smallness. All three Poodles must be of the same basic conformation, and the faults penalized in the breed are heavy build, long back, light, round or prominent eyes, a coarse head, over or undershot jaw and bad carriage or a heavy gait. Soft coats are also frowned upon and any deviations from the accepted coat colours. All solid colours are allowed in the breed, and white or cream poodles must have black noses, lips and eyelids. Brown poodles must have amber eyes and dark liver noses, lips and eyelids. Apricot poodles may have either dark eyes and black points, or deep amber eyes with liver points, and all black, silver or blue poodles must have black points.

The SHIH TZU is a small dog with a large personality, descended from the Apsos of Tibet which were often presented as gifts to the Emperors of China. Known in China as the 'Dog of the Death Dragon', the Shih Tzu has such a profuse coat that it is often difficult to tell which is its head end and which is its tail. The coat is quite easy to keep in good condition despite its length, for it is strong and straight and does not easily tangle. The Shih Tzu is never ill-natured; its temperament is quite perfect and it is bold and sporting, and all these traits combine to make an excellent all-round pet dog.

Left: A salt-and-pepper coloured example of the miniature Schnauzer breed, *Champion Sasupa Careless Fritz of Renlott*.

The Poodle comes in three sizes. Far left is the Standard; below, a family of Miniatures; and right, *Merrymorn Golden Chiffon*, an apricot Toy Poodle.

63

A sweet little grey-and-white Shih Tzu called *Gorseytop Splendid Summer*.

The LHASA APSO is the oldest of the three Tibetan breeds of Utility Dogs and was considered to be the most coveted gift that could be bestowed by the Dalai Lama on his distinguished guests. The little dogs were kept in monastries, and it was said that on death the souls of Lamas entered the bodies of the Apsos, which were therefore accorded the utmost respect. Kept for centuries as treasured pets, it was the alarm bark of the Apso which gave the signal for the great Tibetan Mastiff guards to be released. To this day the breed retains its good qualities as watchdog, for despite his lack of size, he is a bold, courageous and happy little fellow. The name is thought to be a corruption of the Tibetan word for goat, which is *rapso*, for the Tibetan goat has a long and flowing heavy coat, very like that of the little dog. The long coat of the Apso may be golden sandy, honey, dark grizzle, slate, smoke, parti-colour, black, white or brown.

One of the first of the Tibetan breeds to reach Britain was the TIBETAN SPANIEL, having been used for years by the Lamas of Tibet to turn the prayer wheels, by small treadmills, in the temples. Like the Apso, this dog was considered very precious and a suitable gift for a visiting Emperor or King. It is probable that the Tibetan Spaniel is a forebear of the Pekingese, having been taken from Tibet to China and selectively bred in that country for many years. The breed is easy to keep, and the double coat has a silky texture which is quite simple to groom for showing. The face is similar to that of a Pekingese but a little longer in the muzzle, and the eyes less prominent, being oval in shape and wide set. The body is longer than it is high, and the plumed tail is carried in a gay curl over the back. The Tibetan Spaniel may be of any colour or mixture of colours.

The TIBETAN TERRIER was the country dog of Tibet, earning its keep by guarding the caravans, rather than living within the monastery walls. It is a little sharper than the other Tibetan breeds and lives up to the Terrier title; however, this amenable, affectionate little dog makes an excellent pet. Looking rather like a miniature Old English Sheepdog, the Tibetan Terrier has the same square body and upward lift at the quarters, and the same type of profuse coat, which includes lots of long hair falling forward over the eyes. The coat is double and may be of any colour except chocolate or liver.

Tingellan Saucy Sue, an immaculate golden-coloured Tibetian Terrier.

Toy Dogs

The Bichon Frisé is trimmed so as to show its eyes. It may wear some curlers on the way to the show to keep its hair in place. Below is *Ablench Overture of Phieos*, a winning Bichon Frisé dog.

Toy dogs, unlike the other breeds in the non-sporting group, have rarely had any other purpose in life apart from that of providing companionship, and being perfect pets. Sometimes called sleeve dogs, pillow dogs or comforters, these tiny, specially-bred animals were usually the pets of lonely wives, keeping them company while they awaited the return of their husbands from hunting or fighting. As a sleeve dog, the little pet would nestle inside the woman's deep sleeve, an idea copied from the Pekingese sleeve dogs, which spent most of their time tucked into the mandarin sleeves of their masters' garments. As a pillow dog, the Toy would sleep on the pillow at night, and attract any fleas or lice to its own body, which was at a slightly higher temperature than that of its mistress. As a comforter, the little dog would warm his mistress's hands or feet with his natural body warmth. It became very fashionable to have tiny dogs as pets; many notables had their Toys included when having their own portraits painted, and this practice has provided evidence of many of the early versions of today's breeds.

King Charles II was particularly fond of his Toy Spaniels, and these feature in his portraits. Samuel Pepys wrote in his diaries of the time that the King was very fond of his spaniels and spent so much time with them that he neglected affairs of State. It is from these Toy Spaniels that the KING CHARLES SPANIEL of today has been developed. There are four varieties: the Black and Tan, which is most like the original spaniel and called King Charles proper; the Tri-Colour or Prince Charles; the Ruby, which is a rich chestnut red; and the Blenheim, a pearly white with well distributed chestnut patches. The distinguishing feature of this Toy Spaniel is its cushioned-up cheeks.

The other breed descended from the Toy is the CAVALIER KING CHARLES SPANIEL which has a different type of head, and was developed after special prizes were offered for dogs closely resembling those in certain old paintings. The Cavalier is larger than the King Charles with a longer muzzle, but otherwise the two breeds are found in the same colour range and have very similar habits and temperament.

The BICHON FRISÉ is another little dog whose history has been quite easily traced from paintings and portraits of court families, with whom he was a favourite pet and often included in sittings. Although the Toy of today is not identical to those dogs depicted, he is so similar that he must be directly descended from them. Like the poodle and several other curly-coated breeds, the Bichon Frisé was probably bred from the Water Spaniel, or Barbet, being miniaturized by careful selection of breeding stock over the years. This Toy is an attractive dog and his snow-white coat which consists of a mass of loose, silky curls is carefully trimmed to show his eyes, and round off his head.

The tiniest of all the Toys is the CHIHUAHUA, which is found in two varieties, the Long Coat and the Smooth Coat. Both types come in all colours and mixtures. They are dainty, agile dogs with straight fronts and strong hindquarters. The head of the Chihuahua is very round with large, well-flared ears and full, dark or ruby eyes.

Many stories and legends exist to explain the origins of this breed, but it is known that the Spanish who invaded Mexico found ancient Toltec pyramids with carvings of tiny dogs. These exactly resembled the Chihuahua and indicated that the little dog was buried with the dead to lead the way to heaven and to take over its dead owner's sins. Whatever its true history, today's Chihuahua is not only the smallest but also one of the most popular Toy dogs in the world.

Left: An exquisite little cream longcoated Chihuahua, *Deodar Moon Flower*.

Above: The Cavalier King Charles Spaniel is the ideal choice as an undemanding, loyal and affectionate house dog.

Right: *Fleetwards Toybelle*, a delicately coloured blue Italian Greyhound.

The ITALIAN GREYHOUND is identical to the dog faithfully portrayed on many sculptures and friezes dated around 1200 B.C., for he is just a bantamized Greyhound and exactly reproduces that majestic breed's conformation and elegance in miniature. The first examples of this Toy breed arrived in Britain in the seventeenth century, during the reign of King Charles I. They soon became court favourites, retaining their popularity in court circles until well into the reign of Queen Victoria. The breed went into a decline after the Second World War when many specimens were found to be very frail. In Scandinavian countries, slightly larger dogs were bred and encouraged to exercise, and this led to a revival of the breed, with many sound and healthy Italian Greyhounds returning to the show bench. The coat of this miniature Greyhound is extremely fine, covering the skin like satin, and usually needs protection from extreme weather conditions. The dog may be any shade of fawn, white, cream, blue, black, or fawn and white.

The MINIATURE PINSCHER has been bred from indigenous German Terrier types and has very ancient roots. He is not a Toy version of the large Dobermann Pinscher, for 'Pinscher' merely means 'Terrier' in German. The 'Min Pin' was first given recognition in 1895 when the German Pinscher Klub was formed, and great strides were made in the promotion and development of the little dog in the following years. The breed really started its climb to popularity in 1948 when a determined effort was made by fanciers in Britain and the United States to increase the numbers of the Toy on the show bench. The Miniature Pinscher is one of the most soundly made breeds of the Toy Group, sturdy and very muscular, and is willing and able to exercise all day if given the opportunity. He is an excellent guard dog, with good hearing and fast reactions, and as a show dog is the epitome of elegance and style. This breed may be solid red in colour or either black, chocolate or blue with well-defined tan markings according to the breed standard.

Another small smooth-coated Toy Breed is the ENGLISH TOY TERRIER which looks exactly like a miniature version of the Manchester Terrier. In fact the breed does have Championship status in the United States as the Manchester Terrier (Toy). The variety is thought to have been bred from the Manchester Terrier by crossing with the Italian Greyhound in order to reduce size, then selectively back-crossing to retain the distinctive coat colour and type. This Toy dog is always black with sharply defined, rich chestnut-tan markings. The tan colouring must be on the lower legs, and on the long wedge-shaped muzzle, and there should be tan spots over each eye and on each cheek.

This little dog was once used by poachers, being the ideal size and of the right character to put down into rabbit warrens in order to drive the occupants out into the waiting nets. Today he is a rare sight in the show ring, but conducts himself well, and with dignity.

66

The quizzical little
black-and-white
Japanese Chin is
Tueza Taitei.

The JAPANESE CHIN is closely related to the Pekingese and the Pug, and its roots are as ancient as those of its fellow-Orientals, for despite its name, it almost certainly originated in China. The first pair to arrive in Britain were presented to Queen Victoria in 1853, but were considerably larger and coarser than the type seen today. It was not realized in those days that the Japanese valued the tiniest of the breed and only allowed the large specimens to leave the country. Eventually, with out-crosses to other Toys, possibly including the King Charles Spaniel, and with the formation of the Japanese Chin Club, the breed was standardized and has become a firmly established show dog. The 'Jap' has a long and profuse coat completely free of any tendency to wave or curl, with a frill at the neck and a curved, plumed tail. It is either black and white, or any red shade from lemon to brindle, all with white, but tri-colours are not allowed.

The PAPILLON is another dwarf Spaniel, also with Oriental origins. It has been a favourite breed for centuries and has appeared in many paintings by Florentine, Flemish, Dutch, French and English artists. Both Madame de Pompadour and Marie Antoinette are said to have owned Papillons, and the breed was popular in the court circles of Spain, Italy and France.

Once known as the Squirrel Spaniel because of its long curved and plumed tail, the Papillon's present name, which is French for 'butterfly', was coined from the overall appearance of the little dog's head. Its large, upstanding and fringed ears set obliquely on the rounded forehead, which has a narrow white blaze, do look quite remarkably like the delicate wings of a large butterfly.

Though built on slender lines, the Papillon has good bone and is much stronger and tougher than its appearance suggests. The abundant silky coat, which affords the dog perfect protection from both cold and heat, must be white with patches which may be of any colour except liver, symmetrically placed over the head and body. The Papillon is a sound, active dog, always ready to enjoy a game.

The MALTESE is long-coated and snow-white but may have slight lemon markings. It is the oldest of all the European Toy breeds and has a completely unique type of character and conformation. Developed on the island of Malta and referred to by Aristotle and Strabo, the Maltese has remained virtually unchanged for centuries. It was first introduced to Britain during the reign of King Henry VIII and made its debut in the 1860s when dog shows first started. Today the Maltese is a supreme show dog, easily trained and rewarding to prepare. It also makes a delightful and amusing pet, having impeccable manners indoors, and a friendly, attentive nature.

This pert, red Griffon
Bruxellois bitch is
*Shandaff Skibbereen
Mariela.*

The AFFENPINSCHER is one of the oldest Toy dogs of Europe and is a quaint little German breed with a face like a Marmoset. The name translates as Monkey Terrier, *Affe* being the German word for monkey. This dog is probably an ancestor of the Griffon Bruxellois and the Miniature Schnauzer, and is thought to have been originally bred in two sizes, though only the miniature version has survived. The larger type could well have been the Wire-Haired Pinscher, known familiarly as the Rattler at the turn of this century, which is recorded as having been a black dog with a short beard and long whiskers. The Affenpinscher is a rare breed, very tiny and covered with a short, dense coat of black, or black with tan markings, red, grey or other dark colours. The coat is shaggy around the head and neck, and also down the legs. It is an alert and affectionate dog, but can be quite aggressive for its size and so makes a good little guard.

The GRIFFON BRUXELLOIS is probably descended from the Affenpinscher and a mixture of small terriers. It comes from Belgium and was bred with the Pug to produce a smooth-coated variety known as the Petit Brabançon. The Griffon was well established by 1880 but it is thought to have been crossed with Schnauzer and Yorkshire Terrier at that time in order to improve the harsh, wiry quality of the coat and to simultaneously reduce the overall size. The early Griffons were greatly prized by coachmen who liked them for keeping down the rats in the stables, a job they did vigorously and well. Very much a Terrier in body type, the breed has a charming, bewhiskered and moustachioed face to which it is easy to become addicted. The Griffon makes a superb companion for an elderly person, as they are devoted to their owners. His alert and intelligent expression is enhanced by semi-erect, small ears, and large, round and very dark eyes. The coat colours allowed by the show standard are clear red, black or black with rich tan, and in the red, a darker shade on the mask and ears is preferred. The coat has to be hand-stripped for exhibiting the Griffon, but the breed does show well if trained from puppyhood, and allowed to gain confidence.

Pacela Renate of Carmidanick is a fine example of the very ancient Maltese Toy breed.

Right: A tiny and highly intelligent breed of great antiquity is the Pekingese.

Below: *Late Arrival at Furstin* is a quaint and tiny Affenpinscher, deciding not to prick her ears for the camera.

Above: The black Lowchen or 'little lion dog' shown here is *Sonjay Black Magic*.

The PEKINGESE has a history dating back to the Tang Dynasty of the eighth century and is a favourite among the Toy dogs of today. The Chinese Dog of Fo, a deity that guarded the home, was depicted as closely resembling the modern Pekingese, with is broad head, large eyes, deep chest, narrow hips and bowed legs. The breed was brought to Britain in 1860 after the British sacking of the Imperial Summer Palace in Peking. Orders had been given that all the little Lion Dogs were to be destroyed to prevent them from falling into the enemy's hands, but five of the tiny animals were found behind a curtain in the apartments of the Emperor's aunt. She had killed herself but had been unable to kill her beloved pets. The smallest of the five Pekingese was given to Queen Victoria and appropriately named 'Looty', while the other two pairs were kept by the officers who had found them.

The Empress Tzu Hai wrote specific intructions for the dog's breeding and care which still hold true: 'Let the Lion Dog be small, let it wear the swelling cape of dignity around its neck, let it display the billowing standard of pomp about its back. Let its face be black, let its forefront be shaggy, let its forehead be straight and low. Let its forelegs be bent so that it will have no desire to wander far or leave the Imperial Palace. Let its body be shaped like a hunting lion spying for its prey. Let its feet be tufted with plentiful hair so that its footfall may be soundless, and for its standard of pomp let it rival the whisk of the Tibetan Yak which is flourished to protect the Imperial litter from attacks of flying insects.'

Today's Pekingese is a wonderful show dog and a charming pet even though he may be a little strong-willed or perhaps pompous at times, as befits such a distinguished Oriental gentleman with such an impressive history. The long, straight coat is coarse on top but with a thick, soft undercoat. There is profuse feathering on the ears, legs, tail and nose and a thick maning frill of hair round the neck.

Another ancient type of dog is the LOWCHEN, which is said to have

A particularly small example of the popular Toy Yorkshire Terrier.

originated in Russia. Its name means Little Lion Dog, but it should not be connected with the Lion Dogs of the East, for the name refers to the way in which the dog is trimmed. First registered by the Kennel Club in Britain during 1971, the breed proved so popular that it was granted Championship status in 1976. The Lowchen is a sturdy little dog, stronger and broader in the head and body than the Poodle, the breed it most closely resembles. It may be of any colour, white, black and lemon being the most popular, and is a striking, steady show dog.

The YORKSHIRE TERRIER is by far the most popular of all the Toy breeds registered by the Kennel Club in Britain. It has no claim to being an ancient breed, but was developed from other small and diverse Terriers such as the Clydesdale, which is now extinct, the Skye, the Maltese and possibly even the Dandie Dinmont. The first Yorkshire Terriers were far from Toy-sized, and were first exhibited as Broken-Coated Terriers at Leeds in 1861.

During the Industrial Revolution in Britain, many workers moved to the mill towns of Yorkshire, taking with them their small dogs for catching rats and mice in the factories. It is said that the workers' hands became impregnated with natural oils from the fleeces that they handled in the mills and these were transferred to the coats of their Terriers when they stroked them. In the Yorkshire Terrier this gradually improved its appearance by oiling the coat and soon families vied with one another to produce the best groomed little dogs.

Constantly selected for smallness and coat quality, the breed became standardized and much as we see it today. Very much a pampered pet, the Yorkshire Terrier accepts with great poise such indignities as having its coat tied up in paper curlers, and takes every opportunity of proving that he is very much a Terrier, and a real dog despite his diminutive size. The coat of the 'Yorkie' is dark steel blue, and the face and chest a rich tan.

The PUG is unique among the Toy breeds, for whereas most of the others are descended from Terriers and Spaniels, it looks much more like a tiny Mastiff. Once thought to have originated in Holland, due to the fact that early examples were brought to Britain from the Netherlands, it was later considered that they came from China, and were merely transported by Dutch traders. The breed does indeed have the flat face, broad head and prominent eyes found in other Chinese breeds, and old Oriental pictures and pottery show a smooth-coated, straight-limbed little dog, just like the Pug, called the Happa Dog. The origins of the dog's name are also controversial, for some say that it means 'monkey-faced', and others that it is derived from the Latin *pugnus*, meaning a fist.

In China, the Pug's wrinkled brow was considered a sign of great beauty, and the vertical wrinkle was known as the 'prince-mark', being similar to the Chinese character indicating the word for prince. Queen Victoria kept Pugs, and at the end of the last century some black specimens were exhibited at the Maidstone show, creating a great sensation. The standard allows the Pug to be silver, apricot or fawn, all having clearly defined black masks and ears, or the dog may be completely black. A square and cobby little dog, the Pug is well-proportioned and has a distinctive tail which is curled tightly up and over the hip. Very happy in all ways, the Pug makes a good show dog and pet, but is inclined to make snuffling noises and to snore. However, true Pug fans find this endearing.

Scarcroft Coppelia, a fine pug with a well-defined mask.

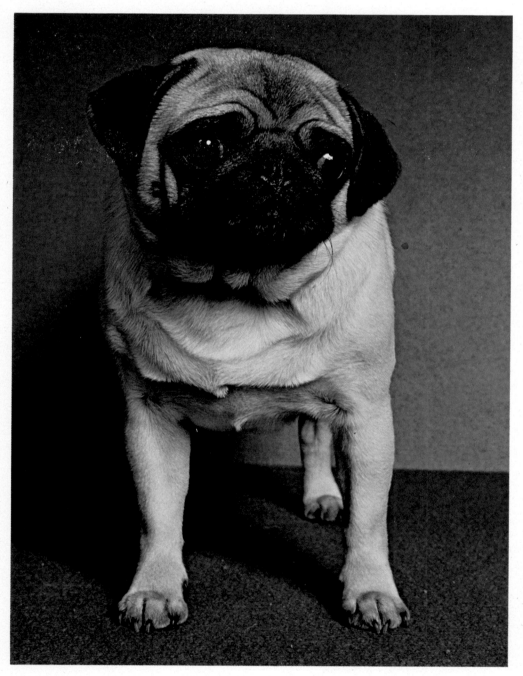

The POMERANIAN is the smallest of the Spitz group, and is descended from the huge sled dogs of the Arctic, being bred down in size from the Deutscher Spitz to the Deutscher Kleinspitz in Pomerania, which is where he received his name. Interim breeds were fairly large and used in herding cattle and sheep, and were generally white in colour. A white German Spitz developed, looking rather like a small Samoyed, and from this the miniature Pomeranian was eventually bred. White was the most fashionable colour for the breed in the early years; now this has been largely superseded by sable and orange, although all whole colours are permitted but must be free from black or white shadings.

The Pomeranian Club was formed in 1891 in Britain and the American Pomeranian Club in 1900. When the first orange 'Pom' was put on the show bench he caused something of a sensation, but his appearance underlined the origins of the breed among northern Spitz dogs, which were the forebears also of the Chow Chow and the Finnish Spitz, often found with clear orange coat colour. Despite its small size, the Pomeranian is still typically Spitz in conformation, with its distinctive skull shape, small, erect, fox-like ears and oval eyes. Its body is short and compact and covered with an abundant coat which stands off the body, and forms a frill or ruff of hair around the neck. The finishing touch is the true Spitz tail, curled up over the back.

The JAPANESE SPITZ is another true Spitz type in miniature, but this time is only found in the pure white form. It was most probably bred from the same root stock as the Pomeranian, when the small white German Spitz was crossed with the Japanese Small Size Dog. This very dramatic Toy dog has considerable charm and character, and looking beautiful prepared for the show ring, may be a top dog of the future.

This is *Ceholms White Osamu of Snowcleve*, a rare Toy dog called a Japanese Spitz.

73

Pet Dogs

Right: In choosing a cross-bred puppy it is important to ensure that it shows no signs of weakness or ill-health.

Above: It is very difficult to decide just what size the cross-bred may be when fully grown, unless both parents are definitely known to the breeder.

CHOOSING A PUPPY

All puppies, whatever their breed, are totally irresistible, and it is wise to spend some time in careful thought before buying one. There are many breeds to choose from as well as mongrels of every shape and size, so there is a dog for every purpose, and a dog to suit every family. Perhaps the best way of seeing lots of dogs in reality is to go along to a local dog show. Here it is possible to see various breeds and to meet dog owners, each of whom will say that his breed is by far the best. When thinking of having a dog it is important to weigh up the disadvantages of each type of breed as well as the advantages. A large and impressive dog takes an equally large and impressive chunk out of the household budget each week, while the very glamorous long-coated varieties need careful grooming and track a lot of dirt into the house during wet weather. Breeds do vary a great deal in their behavioural characteristics. Some are very affectionate, some aloof, some energetic, some very lethargic, some bold, some shy. Some breeds are particularly good with children, others make fearless guards. The list is virtually endless and consideration should be given to breed traits.

Pedigree puppies are best bought from reputable breeders who will be pleased to offer their expert advice in your selection. It is important to buy a puppy with extra good conformation if you intend to show it later, whereas if you merely want a handsome pet, it will not matter whether or not it fails in some minor show points or colouring. The breeder will also advise on which sex would be best to fit in with your family and life style, and give careful intructions regarding exercise, diet, grooming and immunizations. Buying from a breeder also enables you to see the mother of the puppies, and sometimes the father as well, and this may be helpful in forming an idea of the breed's temperament and general demeanour. Breeders of pedigree dogs may be found from advertisements in newspapers and magazines, or by applying to the national Kennel Clubs. It is not generally a good idea to buy from a dealer or market.

When buying a new puppy it is important to choose one that is in good health. Young dogs spend the first few weeks of their lives feeding, sleeping or playing vigorously, so any puppy that sits around looking listless or lethargic is probably feeling unwell. The puppy should have a

This cheeky little dog was the result of crossing two terrier breeds.

This happy little chap is very like a Papillon, but grew to be twice as large as his pedigree mother.

firm, round look, but should not be pot-bellied, with a very round stomach combined with thin hips and a prominent spine, for this may indicate the presence of internal parasites. The skin should be loose and supple and the eyes bright with no sign of any weepiness or matter at the inner corners. The nose should be cool and damp but never wet or discharging, and the tail end should be clean with no sign of the staining which might indicate that it is suffering from diarrhoea. The coat of the puppy should be free of any parasites, and there should be no sore or bare patches on the skin which could indicate the presence of mange or other skin diseases. The ears should be clean inside – dark deposits may mean an infestation of ear-mites. Hernias show as lumps in the navel region or between the hind legs. In the pet dog, these are not serious if very small, but it is unwise to buy any puppy with a large hernia.

If you want your new puppy to grow into a show dog, or intend to eventually breed from it, then even more care must be taken in choice and purchase. Great attention must be paid to the standard of points for the particular breed and the puppy needs checking for correct bone structure, the correct 'bite', i.e. the way in which the teeth meet, and the correct distribution of colour in the coat. It is in the interests of the well-known breeder to help you choose the correct puppy for showing, for his own reputation is at stake, and he would not want a poor specimen on public view in the show ring bearing his registered prefix or kennel name. At the time of purchase, the breeder issues a completed pedigree form, a registration certificate and transfer form so that the puppy may be transferred to the new ownership by the Kennel Club, plus a receipt stating the purpose for which the puppy was bought.

CARING FOR THE NEW PUPPY
A new puppy should be collected as early as possible during the day so that it has plenty of time to explore its new home and to settle down long before nightfall. If the puppy is collected by car the seats of the vehicle should be protected by newspapers topped with an old sheet or towel, as small puppies are frequently travel-sick. If the journey is a long one, it is a good idea to arrange with the breeder to withhold food in the morning

before the puppy starts on its journey, to avoid this sickness.

When the puppy arrives home it should not be over-fussed but given a small and tasty meal. After this its first house-training session should be given by placing the small animal on the earth patch or tray to be used for its toilet purposes. The puppy may have a play pen, or be given the run of the house, or be confined to one room, but in any case it must have its own sleeping box into which it may go whenever it wishes. A cardboard carton is quite adequate as a bed for a puppy, and a convenient size and shape can be chosen and filled with layers of newspapers topped with a washable blanket, sheet or towel.

At this stage the puppy will chew everything within reach, so it is an unnecessary expense to buy it a basket which it may well devour. Because of this chewing habit during teething, great care must be exercised in the home, making sure that electric wires and other potentially dangerous objects are removed from the little dog's play area. Any valuable rugs or expensive shoes should also be placed carefully out of reach. The little puppy may cry for its mother and litter mates at first when left alone, and a stone hot water bottle, well wrapped in an old sweater, may be a comfort.

If the puppy is purchased at about eight weeks of age, it should be taken to the veterinary surgeon for a general health check and to arrange for an immunization programme to commence at the very earliest opportunity. Two injections are usually necessary with a two or three-week interval between them, and consist of combined doses of vaccine against the often fatal canine diseases of hardpad and distemper, canine viral hepatitis and two of the Leptospiral infections.

The veterinary surgeon will also advise on a programme of worming treatments for the puppy. The roundworm is very common in the dog and inhabits the intestinal tract. Almost all puppies are infested with roundworm and need careful and regular doses of medicine to clear them. Tapeworms are less common, but if suspected can be detected by having a sample of the puppy's faeces analysed. At the time of purchase the puppy's breeder will supply a diet sheet, and this should be carefully followed to avoid upsetting the small animal's digestion, and to ensure that it does not lose condition at this critical period in its life. It should be fed at regular intervals, with the correct proportions of food served on clean dishes. Any food left over should be taken away and never left down or fed again later. It is important to have fresh clean drinking water always available in a non-spill bowl.

Puppies get all the exercise they need by playing, but they should be taken out to see as much of the world as possible once they have been completely immunized against disease. Collar and lead training is best started early too, but as the collar will soon be outgrown it is best to start with a comfortable but cheap one which can be replaced when necessary. After wearing the collar in the house for a few days, the puppy will become used to the feel of it, then the lead can be attached and the first lessons in leading may be given. The puppy soon learns its name if this is spoken every time it is called for meals or a game, and it should be taught the meaning of 'No', spoken in a harsh tone, whenever it misbehaves.

All puppies are irresistible, but it is best to select from the whole litter whenever this is possible. Puppies which have had the chance to grow and play in the garden are often stronger and healthier than those bred in confinement.

Overleaf: Two tiny and very sleepy Yorkies.

Above: A very protective Yorkshire Terrier bitch, *Cracker*, and her litter.

As it grows larger, the puppy requires more food but fewer meals, and with the correct care and feeding will grow into a fine dog. Grooming is important for all breeds, the long-coated varieties needing regular brushing and combing to keep the coat free from knots and tangles, and the short-coated dogs just requiring the removal of dead hair and a buffing with a hound glove, or pad of cloth, to tone the muscles and shine the coat. The ears should be checked regularly, and the toenails must be kept trimmed if necessary. An annual veterinary check-up is a good idea, and the immunizations given as a puppy may need an annual or two-yearly booster injection.

A young dog might well benefit from attending obedience classes with its owner, in this way learning to relate to other dogs and to remain calm and controlled in any situation. It is important that a dog receives the correct amount of exercise, and this varies considerably between breeds.

Pedigreed or pet, a properly fed and fit dog is always a credit to its proud owner.

Not all gifts come
Christmas-wrapped.